Jeremiah's Prophecies

THE END OF THE UNITED STATES

CHARLES J. BRANNAN

Printed in the United States of America
Library of Congress Control Number: 2022920939
ISBN: Softcover   979-8-88622-783-3
          eBook   979-8-88622-784-0
Republished by: PageTurner Press and Media LLC
Publication Date: 11/15/2022

To order copies of this book, contact:
PageTurner Press and Media
Phone: 1-888-447-9651
info@pageturner.us
www.pageturner.us

PREFACE

During the years, I have watched the United States go on a downward spiral in its relationship with God. When this country was founded, God was acknowledged throughout the public sector, and his principles were placed in our Constitution. Today, of course, there are people who try to portray our founding fathers as some form of cultist followers with differing views of how they saw God. They leave out the fact that it was from the Bible our schools taught our children when this country was born. There was a harmony between the public and private sectors with God being acknowledged as our true head. Our Congress opened each session with prayer, and that practice continues to this day. We have Moses and the Ten Commandments on display for all to see at the Capitol building where the Supreme Court is housed. To deny there is a Christian heritage in our country and that our forefathers really were not largely fundamental Christians is to ignore all they put in place in this country. Equality of man is a founding principle that comes from God. The freedom we were given in the Bill of Rights stems from theprinciples of God. It is those who do not know God who are today trying to go around the Bill of Rights to establish a new government formed out of their own godless perspective. They are trying to establish a one-party state with them set up as a ruling elite class with all the special privileges they can make available for themselves.

One morning as I was waking up from a night's sleep, God spoke to me and said, "I want you to rewrite the book of Jeremiah and update it for the United States." I immediately said in my heart, "No way!" This was a huge project I knew would be very difficult, and so I was hesitant. After a few weeks, this command I had received from God was still alive in my spirit. I had tried to pass this off as not being from God, but it was obvious by just examining my stubbornness that this command from God was real. I then decided to see if I could get any help in this project, but that was not a good idea. No one was going to help, and this could only be accomplished by one person, just as Jeremiah was the only person that could have written his book more than 2,500 years ago. Finally, I proceeded to write this book, and it was by no means easy, but God gave me the words I needed, which I was free to put on paper using my own style of writing.

This book is a total rewriting of the book of Jeremiah, following it chapter by chapter. God's words for the kingdom of Judah 2,500 years ago were changed to be his words for the United States today. All the warnings God gave Judah are now being passed on to the United States. Jeremiah's message was simple: repent now or be destroyed. Today, God is giving us the same option: repent now or be destroyed. He is calling on his church to turn from its wicked ways and pray. The United States can only avoid God's wrath if God's people will repent and start being active in doing what it takes to save this country from its fast approaching destruction. There is no longer any time left for God's church to sit around idle, letting the wicked rule this country.

It was King Manasseh's long, evil fifty-five-year reign that led God to run out of patience with the kingdom of Judah and declare it was time for their destruction. Even his grandson, Josiah, who was an outstanding king, could not save the kingdom of Judah from God's coming judgment. It was already too late. The people's hearts were removed too far away from God at this point. We are on the brink today in the United States. God is giving us one last chance to get our house in order or the final order for our destruction will be given.

Jeremiah is portrayed in this book as being reborn in spirit to speak to the United States today. He is reliving some of his past and seeing the same things he experienced then coming upon him and to others who share his same vision of coming judgment for this country. Near the end of this book, he turns his attention to some of the other countries today who will soon face God's judgment. The United States is not living in a vacuum, and God's judgment will be passed on to other nations.

This book has been commissioned by God to give his end-time prophecies for what must come to pass in the coming days. The evil spirits that have seized control of other nations are exposed here, and the consequences that will follow can be found in these chapters. One can choose to say, "I have missed the mark on giving God's word for the United States and the other countries in the world, but it would be foolish to think any nation can ignore God's word and practice all the abominations that are carried out today and think God will not bring the judgment he promises will follow."

CHAPTER 1

These are the words of Jeremiah, the son of Hilkiah of the priests that lived in Anathoth in the land of Benjamin: The word of God in heaven came to me in the days of Josiah, son of Amon, who was king of Judah in the thirteenth year of his reign, but has now come to the United States in the twenty-first century through God's timeless words. My words were also spoken in the days of Jehoikim, the son of Josiah, until the destruction of Judah in King Zedekiah's day in 586 BC. These words are God's words for the kingdom of Judah then and the United States today.

God said to me, "Before I formed you in the womb, I knew you, and before you were born, I sanctified you and ordained you to be a prophet to the nations." I answered God, saying, "Oh, my Lord God, I cannot speak to you because I am nothing but a child in your presence." But the Lord answered me, saying, "Do not say you are a child, because you shall go wherever I send you and speak whatever I command you to speak. Do not be afraid of the opposition and disapproval you will facebecause I will always be with you to deliver you from their hands."

Then the Lord put his hand on my mouth and said to me, "Look at what I have done. I have placed my words in your mouth. Notice that this day I have set you over the nations and over the kingdoms to root out, pull down, destroy, and throw down all dark forces that operate here and not only that, but also to build up and plant my words and spirit into this country."

God's word came again to me, saying, "Jeremiah, what do you see?" I answered, "I see a rod formed from an almond tree." Then God said, "That is right. This rod represents my promise, that I will rapidly enforce my word to bring it to pass." Then God, for a second time, said to me, "Jeremiah, what do you see?" I answered him, "I see a pot that is seething, facing toward the north." God answered me, "From the north, an evil shall break forth upon this land. An evil is coming to the United States, which shall affect every inhabitant in this country. I will call the demonic forces from the nations to pour out into the United States and set up places to rule everywhere in the United States. Every city will have a demon in charge of it and subject to it. Why is this happening? It is happening because my judgment has come upon this country as a result of your wickedness. You in the United States have forsaken Me. You have worshipped your gods of pleasure, money, and other things and have forgotten Me. You have sat in your churches, playing church but have never spent any time to know Me. Jeremiah, rise up without fear and speak what I command you to speak. Do not let anyone intimidate you from speaking my word, or my protection will be lifted from you. Today you are a high wall, an iron pillar, a defended fortress against the present-day rulers of this country: the silent church, the media, and the ignorant souls of the United States. They will fight you to defeat my word coming through you, but they will not prevail against you because I am always with you to deliver you."

CHAPTER 2

Moreover, God spoke to me, saying, "Go and speak to this nation, saying, 'You, the United States of America, I remember you when I established you, how you sought Me and filled my word throughout your society. You acknowledged Me in your Declaration of Independence and put my principles in your Constitution. You were holy to Me in your birth, and I defended you against your enemies. Evil has come upon all who have fought against you. Hear Me now! My question to you who live in the United States is, what sin have you found in Me to cause you to abandon Me? You have left Me so you could walk after vain things. You have become vain. None of you have asked, "Where is the Lord that established us? Where is he that defended us from all enemies and gave us a land of plenty?" I brought you into this land to give you freedom to worship Me. It was a new land free from the restrictions of the old land. However, now you have defiled the land I have given you and abandoned Me. My ministers and those I put in charge of my church have not noticed I am no longer among them.

They have sinned, polluting my word by mixing it with what the world desires. All these things they have done have been to their harm and not profit. Therefore, I will plead with you once more and also plead with your grandchildren to look out at the other countries and see if this has ever happened. Has any nation ever changed its gods for those who are no gods? However, you have changed from the honor I have given you to that which does not profit.' Oh heavens, be astonished at what has happened and be afraid for what is about to come to pass. The people of the United States have committed two evils. They have forsaken Me, their creator, their fountain of sustenance, and have gone after vain things that will lead to their destruction.

"Has the United States become a slave? Does he serve other countries? Why has he been laid waste by other countries? His enemies have come and spoiled him, destroying his cities with fire and leaving him with no inhabitant. Those countries have broken your power, leaving you powerless. Have you not brought this upon yourself because you have forsaken the God who created you and guided you from your founding? Can you succeed partaking of the pollution of those countries you depend on? Your own wickedness shall punish you. Your backslidings shall cause Me to reprove you. You better take notice that it is an evil and unpleasant thing you have done in leaving Me to follow your sins. You do not acknowledge or honor Me anymore.

"Since your beginning, I gave you your freedom and you honored Me by seeking my favor, but you continually strayed from Me. I nourished you and gave you a land of plenty, but now you are twisted and corrupt. I do not know you. No matter how much you justify yourself and say you are pure, I have your sin marked down where it cannot be forgotten. How can you say, 'I am not polluted, I am a Christian nation,' when you are blind? Do you not know what you have done? You have lived your lives without honoring Me. You have lived as though I were a trivial part of your life. You think you can call on Me at any time when you have ignored Me at all other times. You have said you do not want to be encumbered by my standards and you will seek whatever suits your pleasure. When a thief has been discovered and becomes ashamed he has been caught, so now are all people of the United States. They, their rulers, their pastors, and priests have now become ashamed before the God of heaven. They have put their dependence on their money and all they spend their time on and have totally discarded Me from their lives. They have turned their backs on Me and expect Me to hear them when they get in trouble and call on Me. Where are your gods you have put above Me? Let them save you in your time of need if they can save you. You have put as many gods before you as there are cities in your country. Why will you plead with Me to save you? You have sinned and left Me.

It has been for nothing that I corrected your children when they went astray. They do not receive correction today. You have attacked the very people I have sent to point out the sins you are committing. Have I been a cancer to you for you to cast Me aside while saying you are your own gods and will not listen to Me anymore? Can a bride forget her wedding dress the day of her marriage? Yet, you have forgotten Me days without number. Why have you pursued your own desires without Me? By doing this, you have taught others your wicked ways. The blood of those who have stood against your sin and of those unborn children you have killed for pleasure-seeking has not been unnoticed. You think you are innocent before Me and that I will not punish you. You think you have my approval for what you have done because my pastors have said it was okay. Why are you trying to argue with Me that you are righteous? You were ashamed of these things in the past, and you will be ashamed again. You will not be able to use your excuses to claim your innocence before Me. You have rejected my principles, and it will lead to your ruin."

CHAPTER 3

"It is said if a man divorces his wife and she goes and marries another, shall he be allowed to return to her? Such a thing is an abomination to Me. However, you have played the harlot with many lovers and continue to return to Me. Look intently at all you have done and see with whom you have been sleeping. You have played the whore and filled the land with your wickedness. Therefore, your land has suffered drought, earthquakes, tornados, hurricanes, and other storms of great magnitude while you refuse to be ashamed of your actions. Will you not continue to cry to Me for the protection of your land? Do you think I will withhold my anger forever? Will I hold off my punishment for the end of time? Look and see, you have done all the evil you could ever imagine to do."

The Lord continued, "Have you seen what is happening in the United States? This country has left Me in pursuit of its gods of pleasure, money, and religion. It is playing the harlot with its gods. I told this country after it did all these things to repent and come back to Me. This country has refused to come back to Me. It has refused to take notice of my warnings of September 11, 2001. My church has seen this and has failed to heed my warnings by remaining silent. This country has turned away from Me, divorcing itself from Me, and so I have divorced it. My church could have changed things in this country to save it but has remained silent. It has turned to its religious practices, thinking that somehow I am satisfied with ceremony. My church only lightly esteems Me today. The United States, with all its carnality, has justified itself more than my church."

God said, "Go and shout these words throughout the country,

'Everyone, turn back to the God who brought this country into existence!' If you do this, I will not pour my wrath out upon you because I am a God of mercy. I will not stay angry at you forever. I just ask you to acknowledge your sin. Admit you have sinned against Me and turned Me aside after your other gods. Acknowledge you have disobeyed Me.

"I am telling all of you to turn back to Me. You have gone astray. I have been married to you. I created you, and want to bring each of you back to the relationship we once had. I will restore to you pastors and priests who will minister to you my truth. They will give you the knowledge and understanding you no longer have. When you begin to prosper again, all the things you have depended on before will be forgotten and removed. You will have a fresh start. Once again, you will be the seat of the gospel for the world, and my Holy Spirit shall roam again through your land. You will not be seeking those evil things with which you once filled up your lives. My church and the government will no longer be in enmity with each other. You will not have to question how I will do this. Just know that I have said you will honor Me, as your forefathers did, once again. You will trust Me once again as the cornerstone of this country.

"Just as anyone who commits treachery against another, you have been treacherous to Me. It is being whispered in countries around the world how the United States has departed from the God in whom it trusted. It has turned to its idols and forgotten that it was God who gave it all it possesses. People of the United States, return to Me, and I will heal your land. I will pardon your sins. You have to turn to Me because I am your only salvation. Your land yearns for my salvation. It is in constant unrest and turmoil because you have abandoned Me. I am your salvation. Blood is on your hands, casting a veil over your entire country. This shame of guilt envelops you, leaving you in confusion. You have sinned against Me from your founding and have not obeyed the words that I have imparted to you."

CHAPTER 4

"If you will return to Me and turn from your wicked ways, then I will not bring an end to your country. If you will confess that I am the God on whom you have been founded, judge righteous judgments and stop espousing your lies one to another, then you shall be a blessing to all nations and will witness my glory to all others in the world. Understand, you must reject those things that have caused you to turn away from Me. Do not seek those things that do not profit your lives. You must cleanse your hearts of the evil that is in them unless you want my fury to come on you like a raging fire that cannot be controlled. It cannot be controlled because of the sin you have enjoyed pursuing in defiance of Me.

"I want all in my church and all in the media to proclaim to the world, saying, 'Fear now what is coming upon you.' Flee now because a terror is coming upon your land. Evil and great destruction shall roll across this land. The seed of your destruction is at the door to lay waste your country, touching every life. Weep now and moan for the judgment of God coming to destroy your land. When this day comes, your president and all your leaders in the government and the church shall be dumbfounded. All of your prophets will be perplexed." I then said to God, "Surely you have deceived the people of this country in telling them that they will live in an era of peace when there is actually a sword ready to pierce them through the heart." God answered, "A foul wind is blowing in from the countryside that cannot cleanse or cool those who are hot. It is a wind that brings searing heat and drought. It will sweep across this country to oppress all in it. You can see my judgment coming to you in the sky. It is an omen of swift destruction. All of you must turn from your wicked ways so that I can save you from what is coming. How much longer will you keep on running after your evil desires? A voice is announcing for all to hear in this land and throughout the whole world that the enemy is at the door, speaking its desires against this country. This enemy is ready to pour into your land from all sides because you have rebelled against Me. All the evils you have done have brought this judgment on yourselves. All of this evil has been deeply rooted in your hearts.

"Oh, how I wish I do not have to bring judgment upon you, but the alarm has been sounded. The enemy has been spotted. He is coming. People are wailing for the destruction that has been inflicted on the land. Everyone's possessions have been spoiled. How long will the enemy spoil our land? The people of this country are foolish. They have never known Me. They behave like spoiled children who have no concept of a parent's correction. They are well instructed on how to pursue their evil desires but have no idea how to live righteously.

"In the beginning, I beheld the earth I created. It had no form and there was a void between it and the heavens. There was no light. I looked at the mountains and they began to shake, and the hills also trembled lightly. There was no man, and the birds had flown away. The fruitful valley was a wilderness and all the cities had been leveled because of my fierce anger. Know for a surety this land shall be laid waste, but I will not leave it totally destroyed. Those who depended on this country will mourn, and the sky will be dark, because I have spoken it into existence through this word, and I will not change my mind about what I am going to bring to pass in this country.

"Everyone in the cities shall fear and flee from the noise of destruction racing toward them. The cities shall be emptied of all inhabitants because of what is rapidly approaching. When you have lost all your possessions, what will you do? Even if you put makeup on your face and don your best attire, it will not impress those who seek your life. I have heard the voice of a woman in labor bringing forth her first child in all the pain she is suffering, declaring out loud, 'I cannot bear it anymore. I am dying and there is no remedy.'"

CHAPTER 5

"Run through your neighborhoods and search the countryside and see if you can find anyone that espouses truth or seeks righteous decrees, and I will pardon your sin that brings judgment upon your land. Although you say you are a Christian nation, you do not really believe it. You ask if I am the source of truth. You have seen my punishments for your sins but have remained unrepentant. You refuse to be corrected by Me. You have taken a stand, saying, 'I will not return to the God that this country once loved.' Therefore I have stated you are poor, miserable souls who are so foolish you cannot recognize my ways or the judgment that looms over your heads.

"So I will go and converse with your great men, those who have had a relationship with Me and have understood my ways. They have understood what it is to be free. They have tasted my blessing. However, a beast from afar shall come and slay them. The predators of the night shall lay waste your land. Those who seek your life will lie in wait in your cities like a spider waiting for its prey to capture anyone straying outside. All of this will come to you because you have disobeyed Me and desire Me no more. Your sins are so many. They cannot be numbered at all. How can I pardon you for all you have done? Your children have forsaken Me and embraced atheism, never recognizing that the food they eat comes from Me. They have committed adultery against Me with their gods. They go in droves to the pleasure palaces. They have been insatiable lechers who seek out their neighbors' wives. Shall I not punish you for this? Shall I not bring my judgment on such a nation as this?

"Go and destroy this nation. Leave nothing for it to use to defend itself. Do not totally destroy everything, but clear out all that offends Me. This must happen because this country and my church have betrayed Me, turning to other gods. They have lied about Me, saying I have not spoken any judgment to come on this country. They have said there will be no judgment, there will be no famine or drought, there will be no enemy to destroy us. All the prophets who proclaim this are bags of air with no power in their voices. I will turn their words against them. Because you have said these things, I will bring power with my words against you to consume you. You will perish like wood placed in a fire. I will bring a nation against you from afar, a people whose language you do not understand. They are a mighty nation filled with mighty men that will consume all that you have produced. They shall go through your countryside, taking everything from you that you possess. You will be defenseless against them because you will give up your defenses to them. However, know that you will not be totally destroyed.

"You ask Me, 'Why did this happen to us?' My answer to you is because you have abandoned Me and served your gods of pleasure, money, and religion. So if you want to serve these gods, then I will let you do it in a place that is not yours. You will be removed from your homes. Hear this now! Let it be published throughout the whole earth. Foolish Americans, who cannot see with their eyes, hear with their ears, or understand anything I say to them. Do you believe Me or not? Can you stand against the one who formed the seas and the dry land, telling the sea it can go no farther than the shoreline? You have been in rebellion against Me. You have hardened your hearts against Me. You no longer honor Me among others as the one who has given you the rain in its time for your crops and made your land the envy of the world for its productivity. Your sins have brought all this to an end. All the blessings I have imparted to you will not be imparted to you anymore. Your church leaders are wicked men disguised as godly men. They set traps to ensnare as many as they can to join them in their sin. They have deceived those who come to them in order to make themselves rich. They love the praise of men and fame. They have overindulged themselves and given excuses to all that this sin is okay because God's word is not inerrant. They play favorites with those from whom they expect to receive and curse those who have nothing. They care only for their own prosperity and cast aside any who come to them with real need.

"Shall I not punish you for all this? Shall I not avenge those whom you have cast aside? Shall I not judge this nation for casting Me aside? A remarkable and horrible judgment is coming on this land. My pastors and preachers have prophesied lies to my people, and my people do not want to hear the truth. They love the lies, and yet there shall be a consequence for denying the truth."

CHAPTER 6

"People of this country, prepare to flee from your cities. An alarm is being sounded about an evil that is coming from afar into this country to bring great destruction. This country is like a defenseless woman surrounded by those who want to ravish her. They shall encircle her, leaving her no escape. They wait and make plans to take her. They wait for the dark to grab her and rape her. Build your siege towers against the United States. This is the country I want punished because of the oppression the government has wrought on its people. This government has cast its oppression on all, causing its citizens to mourn. Day and night, my people cry out to Me for justice. I speak to the United States government with my warning that when I remove my protection from you, your land will be laid waste, leaving you with no inhabitant to control. My people you seek to control will be removed from your grasp. Who among you can hear my voice? Your spirit is dead within you and cannot fathom my existence. You cannot possibly hear Me or hearken to my warnings because my word is an abomination to you.

As a result, I am full of fury against you. I am tired of holding back my judgment. All your citizens abroad and the youth you have tried to fill with your propaganda will not escape my fury. The poor and the rich, the powerful and the basest of citizens, the old and the young shall all feel my fury.

"Your houses and your land shall be given to others. Your spouses shall be taken from you. My hand of judgment will stretch out over the entire country. From the most powerful of your citizens to the basest of your citizens, all have given themselves over to malicious desires. Even my pastors and priests and those in authority in the church have been practicing their sins in the dark. They have been saying to my sheep in the church that a day of judgment will never come. They want them to believe that things in this country can continue as they are. Have they never been ashamed of their actions? No, they have never been ashamed. They consider it an honor to live in their sin. My clergy and its leaders shall not escape my judgment on this nation. I will remove them from their offices. Remember the past when people heeded Me and followed my commandments. They sought Me, looking for the peace that passes understanding, and yet you say you will not consider listening to Me today. I have given you church leaders in the past to be the watchmen for your souls and have sent others today to warn you of coming judgment, but you reject all their warnings, saying, 'We will not listen to you, God!'

"Therefore, I want everyone throughout the world to know I will bring destruction upon the people of the United States. Their evil desires and the sins they love to pursue shall bring my wrath on this nation because they have rejected my commandments and my words of warning to them. Those in my church keep practicing their religion every Sunday, thinking I am pleased with one hour of acknowledgment. The pastors and priests lead my flock through their ceremony, thinking they are touching my heart. Your ceremony and your weekly acknowledgment of Me are a stench in my nostrils. I will lay traps before your steps and your family will step into them. Your neighbor and your friend will perish. Seriously consider that a powerful country is coming against this nation that will encircle you. They will pass judgment on this nation and will not show mercy. They are coming with their armies to enslave you. You will be in terror because of their power, and you will have nowhere you consider safe to run. I call on my people to call out to Me and repent, because a dire judgment is coming upon this nation. This judgment is rapidly approaching. I have set you, Jeremiah, as a beacon of light to those who can heed my voice. You are the one I have chosen to send out the words of salvation to them. The people of this country have rebelled against Me as their leader. They lie and slander others, and their hearts are hearts of stone filled with their detestable desires. This land has become desolate because of the wicked in it. The wicked have been elected to power and the people of the country want it this way. I, the Father of mankind, reject those who have led this country to ruin."

CHAPTER 7

God spoke to me and said, "Stand in the center of your capitol and let the people know I am saying to turn away from your sins now, and I will not take this land away from you. Do not put your trust in those who are lying to you, hinting you have nothing to fear because you have put In God We Trust on your money. If you truly turn from your wicked ways and begin to execute true justice to all; if you end your oppression of those who hold no political office; if you stop your slaughter of the innocents; if you turn away from your gods of money, sex, religion and power; then, I will not remove you from the land for which your forefathers fought.

"Up until now, you have believed all the lies your leaders have been telling you. They are empty words meant to entice you. Will you continue to lie, steal, and murder to serve your gods you have placed above Me to satisfy that hunger in your soul? Will you stand before Me to claim you are free to do as you please? Has my church in this country become so corrupt it cannot recognize that mingling with the world's morals is an abomination in my eyes? Do you really think I have not noticed the compromises you have made with my word? Look at the past countries who forgot about my laws and did as they pleased, and observe their end result. Nazi Germany tried to destroy my people of Israel, and its people paid a heavy price. As I did to them, so will I do to you. There will be no friend or ally you can turn to for help. No one who utters a prayer of intercession for you will be heard. It is too late to turn back my judgment. I will refuse to hear any prayer on your behalf. Look at what is being done in secret in your cities. You are spending all your time trying to satisfy your evil heart with unmentionable practices. You have ignited a fire of wrath to come against you that cannot be put out. Have not all these practices of yours caused you to dig your own graves?

"Therefore I am giving you a final warning: my wrath will be poured out on this nation. No person, animal, or fruit of your field will escape my punishment. I will burn it all with a cleansing fire. Those in my church can continue to serve Me feignedly. All their services, meetings and ceremonies mean nothing to Me. Have I ever told any of you this is how I wish to be worshipped? The thing I have told you to do is to obey Me. Obedience is better than sacrifice. You cannot cleanse the flesh. Obey Me, and I will be your God, and you shall be my people. If you walk in the ways I have told you, then my blessings will fall on you and not my curses. Instead, you have chosen to close your ears to my words. You have walked after your own evil desires. You continue to walk backward and not forward.

"Since your founding, I have sent you the ministers to lead and guide you on that narrow path so many find it difficult to walk. All that I have done to guide you has failed to stop you from walking into that path of destruction. Through the years, you have hardened your ears and your hearts so that you can no longer hear my voice. You are filthy rags to Me in comparison to your forefathers. Jeremiah, despite all these warnings you will give them, they will not hear you. They will shut their ears and not listen. They have no words to answer you because they love their sin too much. Nevertheless you shall say to them, 'This is a nation that will not obey the God of heaven. They refuse to be corrected. The truth is something that is foreign to them.' Take the blinders off your eyes, America, and begin to weep and mourn over My judgment to come. I have removed my presence from you, and with the absence of my presence comes my wrath.

"The political and religious leaders of this country have done evil in my sight. My church has come in agreement with the evil laws enacted in this nation. They have let the government glorify the perverted, unnatural practices my word testifies against. It has silently let my unborn children be murdered. None of this could have ever come into my mind to allow such a thing as this. All the graves that have been dug for those who have been slaughtered shall make room for those who have allowed this slaughter to take place. Your flesh shall be eaten by the birds. No one will fray them away. There will be no more joy in your cities. There will be no more parties in which to go. Your land will be desolate."

CHAPTER 8

"When all this occurs, all the graves of your important men will be opened and their bones exposed. All the secrets they hid in their life will be revealed for the whole earth to know how they served their gods of pleasure, money, and fame. All this will be revealed to their shame to destroy the legacy they tried to build. All those who have followed their footsteps to be like them will end up choosing death rather than life. I will drive them to places they will not wish to go. You may ask if I will ever let them rise again to the heights of fame they once had. Will I ever let them return to their former station in life? The answer can be contained in the question: why do these people continue to run after their sins? They cling to their deceits and refuse to hearken to Me. I have listened to them and heard every deceitful word that has come out of their mouths. Not one of them has repented for his sins but only continues to say they are innocent victims of slander. They have rushed headlong into the disaster that awaits them. The migrating birds know when it is time to leave. The butterfly knows when it is time to depart, yet the people of this country cannot recognize that the time of my judgment for their sins is upon them.

"How can you say you are righteous before Me and walk in my commandments? Without doubt, all my warnings to you have been in vain. Your educated elite have become dismayed and frightened. They have rejected Me as insignificant, saying it is foolish to consider Me as Creator. Therefore, I will take your spouses and estates from you and give possession of them to others. They shall inherit what was once yours. From the greatest of you to the least, all of you have abandoned Me to chase after your sins. My ministers in the church and those I have gifted with prophecy have deceived my people about what is rushing toward them. They have continued the lie of saying, 'Peace and good times are coming to America.' There is no peace coming to America but a time of war. Have they been ashamed of their sin? No, they have not been ashamed of their sin. Therefore, they shall not escape what is coming to America. They too will be crushed by the enemy that is coming. Everything my servants have done to deceive my people will swiftly bring my wrath on them. All that they possess and have worked for will be taken from them."

The people will say, "Why are we sitting still? Come, it is time to find places of safe haven to escape God's wrath. We must hide in our holes and be quiet in hope that God will not find us and finish the judgment he has passed on to us. Our sin has been found out, and we must hide from his wrath. We expected there to be peace, but instead there has been war. We have looked for prosperity, but instead there has been dearth." God said, "Behold, the enemy has been spotted. He is coming with a full force to crush all in his wake. Every city and town is being laid waste before him. I am sending serpents into your cities that cannot be charmed. They will inject you with their poison, leaving you nowhere to hide.

"The pain in my heart for all I must bring on you is terrible. My people are crying from the countries they have fled to, asking, 'Has God truly abandoned America? Has its government really fallen?' Why has this nation provoked Me to such fury that I have to destroy it? Their sins are so many, I cannot overlook them. The time of salvation has passed. The end of the harvest is over. The pain I feel over the destruction of this country is like a sore that cannot be healed. Astonishment has taken hold of Me. There is no medicine to heal my people. There is no doctor who can heal this disease."

CHAPTER 9

"If it were only possible for Me to cry for the people of this country, I would cry. I see their lifeless bodies strewn across the countryside. If I only had a place on earth I could send all the wicked of this country so their evil could not spread through the earth, I would do it. There sins are so many, they cannot be numbered. Their treachery and lust fill the earth. Every word they speak is a lie. They do not know how to speak the truth. They commit one sinful act after another, because that is all they know to do. They have never known Me. Do not trust your neighbor. Do not put your confidence in your brother. Each of them will stab you in the back and speak slanders against you. Every person will practice his lies against his neighbor. None will speak the truth. All will rise up in the morning and go to bed at night filling their entire day with unrighteous acts. Their habitat is one where deceit is fully practiced. All refuse to accept Me as their God. Therefore, I give my warning: I will set them before my judgment seat and put them on trial for their sins. What other option do I have, since I am a God of justice?

"Every word that comes out of their mouth is full of deceit. One speaks to his neighbor words of peace. Meanwhile he is plotting against him waiting for a time to strike. Shall I not punish these people for their sins? Shall I not pour out my wrath on this nation? I will weep for the land that has been polluted by the people of this country. I will send words lamenting the meadows and mountains I placed here. All of this has been burned and become a wasteland. There is no sound of the cattle in the field and the birds in the trees. They have fled the destruction that has ravaged the countryside. I will level your cities and leave you without shelter. This land shall be barren, and your cities will be empty. Who is wise enough to understand what is coming? Who will I send to warn the people who live in this country of the destruction that is near? Who will be able to declare that everything will be destroyed by fire, driving out all inhabitants?

"Because you have rejected my commandments and hidden them in your closets and storerooms, you will feel my wrath. Because you have purposely chosen to disobey Me and walked after every carnal desire filling your hearts, you will know my justice. Your parents have raised you to follow them in their sin. Your reward for following them will be the cup filled with my wrath that you will be forced to drink.

"I will drive you from your homes and send raiding parties after you to finish you off. I will take the last of your possessions from you. I will call on my followers who have been scattered by the enemy to weep for this country. With urgency they must plead with Me to withhold any further judgment. I hear them praying, 'Why has the enemy spoiled us? We are perplexed because our land has spewed us out. We have no homes in which to dwell.' Yet hear Me, my people. Teach your children how to cry. Teach your neighbor how to lament for this country. Death has come to this country. Death is found everywhere in your streets.

Your children and your young men have all been slain. The dead are strewn across the countryside with no one around to bury them. This is the future for those who reject Me.

"No wise man may glory in his wisdom. No mighty man may glory in his might. No rich man may glory in his wealth. You may only glory in that you know Me. I delight in those who love their neighbor and seek to do righteous acts. I love righteous judgments and will cast out those who make unrighteous decrees.

"Let my people beware. Those who say they know Me will be punished with those who do not. I have no favorites when sin is in my house. All will face my wrath. The chaff must be burned with a cleansing fire."

CHAPTER 10

"Listen to Me now! I am speaking to you, America. Do not follow the heathens' example, those who do not know Me. Do not become dismayed at the signs from heaven like the heathen always do. Their customs are futile. They cut down a tree to make paper money and begin to worship it. This paper cannot talk. It cannot grow legs and walk. It is nothing to be feared because there is no good or evil in it. I am the one to be feared. I am the one full of might. Who would dare to not fear Me? No one can compare to Me. No one can stand up to Me. But the heathen are full of foolishness. They are so full of themselves, they cannot see beyond their noses. Everything they believe is as an empty vessel. Everything they esteem as important has been manufactured by another man. Fear the one who fashioned the earth. I am the one true God. I am an everlasting king whose kingdom will know no end. My wrath shall make all nations tremble. No nation can withstand my judgment.

"All the things you have made with your hands shall perish. They are not eternal. I am the eternal one who created the heavens and the earth. It is through my wisdom the universe holds together. The rain on the earth falls at my command. The storms in store are released at my discretion. Every man is wise in his own eyes and yet has no knowledge. Each one trembles before the idols he has created in his own life. Those idols have no breath or life in them, and they shall one day perish. What I have given to you is life and the fulfillment of your desires. All is mine, and you can inherit from Me. Gather up your possessions now while you can. Those who are not ready will be flung out of this land. My judgment is following you like a mad hornet.

"I am hurting so much for what must come to pass. The judgment that is coming grieves my heart. My churches have been spoiled. Those who were in them have left, nowhere to be found. My pastors have put blinds in front of their eyes and no longer seek Me. Poverty shall overtake them, and all they have will fall out of their grasp. The sound of the enemy can now be heard. They are coming to ransack all this land's cities."

I prayed, "O Father, I know man does not possess the ability to walk uprightly. He is unable to order his own steps. My God, chasten me according to my sins. Cleanse me from my imperfections. Do this out of your love for mercy and not out of your anger. Your anger destroys, while your mercy brings cleansing. Pour out the cup of your wrath on the heathens who do not know you and on their families who deny your existence. It is their hatred and violence that has been inflicted on your people."

CHAPTER 11

God's word came to me, saying, "Hear the promises I have made to the people of this land. Relay all my words to them. A curse shall be on everyone who breaks my law. I bestowed my blessings on you in your beginning in exchange for your vows to obey Me. As long as you obey Me, I will keep my presence among you and my blessings on you will know no end. I gave you a land of plenty that has sustained you all these years. I sealed it with a promise that no adversary could amend. Jeremiah, shout the words of my favor on the United States and remind them to turn to Me with all of their heart and obey my commandments. I have constantly from your founding to this day commanded you to observe my laws, and yet after all my blessings on this country I have been ignored. Everyone in this country pursues all the evil he can produce from his own heart. Because you have done this, then I must remove my blessings from this nation and release my curses upon it.

"I have examined the hearts of the people in this country and found a conspiracy to follow the sins of their forefathers and to remove Me from their presence. They all wish to cling to their sins like scales to a serpent. Since this is where you have positioned your hearts, then an evil is coming upon you from which you cannot escape. Although you may cry and call out to Me for mercy, I will not hear. Then you will turn to the gods you have made in your hearts and search for deliverance from them, but it will be to no avail. Your gods you have created will not be able to save you. The number of idols you have in your life is as numerous as the cities you have in your nation. All of you sacrifice to these idols you have set up in your hearts by depending on them for your livelihoods and never considering Me.

"There will be no prayer of deliverance for this people because I will refuse to hear such prayers. Although they will cry out to Me with buckets of tears, there can be no forgiveness without repentance. Why have the sheep in my church turned from Me? Why have they embraced the world's values into my church? You have rejoiced in your evil and caused my Holy Spirit to leave your congregations. In your beginnings, you were the joy of my heart, but now you are rottenness in my bones ready to be cut off my tree. This country shall not escape my wrath. Your punishment awaits you because of your service to your gods."

God showed me there has been a plot devised against my life. Their wicked hearts want to stop God's words against this country from being delivered. I have no power against them. I can only call out to God for his protection. I know he tries men's hearts and sees their evil devices. He will turn their own plans against them because I am righteous before his eyes. The people who want to stop God's word from reaching this nation say, "Do not speak and write these prophecies against this country—if you do, you will face our justice. We will stop this word." God answered, "I will punish all of you for your defiance. Your sons and daughters shall be taken from you. They will perish in the drought and famine I will bring upon this land. Your words against those who deliver my warnings to this country will bring my judgment on you and your families."

CHAPTER 12

I began talking with God, saying, "Lord, you are righteous, and by your standards I must plead my case. I ask you about your justice. Why do you allow the wicked to prosper? Why are they allowed to live lives of pleasure while practicing their treachery? You gave them their existence, they grew up to be adults and have prospered. You have always been near enough for them to call on you, but they have chosen to keep you always at arm's length. Despite all this, you know me and know my works. You have examined my heart toward you. Have no mercy on them, Lord. Judge them according to their sins. Prepare them for your day of vengeance. How long shall our land mourn and suffer the consequences of this people's wickedness? Our crops have suffered damage, our meat for food has been totally consumed. We are all in dire straits because this nation believes there will be no consequences for its sins.

"If one cannot win a race against a slow runner, how can he race against a horse? If this nation has no money to wage war in a time of peace, what will it do in a time of war? Father, even your church has turned against you with its treachery. It has called on the world into joining it into defying your words. Do not listen to its lies when it wraps them up in devotionals."

God replied, "I have removed my spirit from this church. I have left it defenseless against the enemy that is coming. Because the church in this country has cried out against my laws, I can no longer protect them. This church is as an unacceptable sacrifice to Me. I call on the enemy to come in like a flood and devour it. Many of my pastors have led my flock astray. They have taught them a doctrine that is foreign to Me. My churches are full of lost souls who have never received the gospel inside their walls. There is mourning throughout the land because my gospel is no longer preached. There is no foundation of my word in the people of this country to save them from my judgment. All these houses of worship for Me will be destroyed. A war against this apostate church will be waged, leaving it to know no peace. This church has sought material gain but will reap poverty. The people in this church have sought to earn their way into heaven but will learn it is not by works. All the wealth and material objects this church has coveted only bring my wrath upon it.

"I am letting those across the world who have anxiously waited for the destruction of the United States know I will carry out my punishment on this country. I will scatter them from this land. After I have judged them, I will have compassion on them. I will restore those who have been cleansed to their homes. All those who inhabit this country who came from afar during this cleansing will be allowed to stay and learn of Me. If they obey my word and do not depart from my laws, then they shall prosper. However, if they will not obey, I will once again judge this land."

CHAPTER 13

The Lord spoke to me, saying, "Put on an undergarment and wear it, and then take it to the Euphrates and bury it in the rocks, marking where you have placed it." So I did as the Lord commanded me. After many days had passed, the Lord said to me, "Go back to the Euphrates and uncover the undergarment you hid in the rocks." So, once again, I did as the Lord instructed me. I went to the river and found the undergarment and marked how it was ruined. It could not be worn again. Then God spoke to me and said, "Just as this garment has been ruined lying next to the Euphrates, so will I soil the pride of the United States and its government. The evil people in this country and those who lead them will be thrown down into the mire with all their power stripped from them. This is their due reward for running after every perverse desire that fills their hearts, following after gods I never gave them.

"It has always been my desire to bless this nation and its people. I have wanted that close relationship with them as a husband has with his wife, but they have rejected Me. Therefore, I will give them all a bottle of wine filled with my wrath to drink. I will make every citizen and ruler of this country as well as every official of my church to drink this bottle filled with my wrath. Each one will become drunk with the punishments that are to come. They all will be cast into a den of hungry lions to be consumed with no mercy or pity coming from Me. Father and son, mother and daughter will all be thrown into the den together. Remove your pride from yourselves and give glory to Me before I place you into darkness, causing you to stumble over the rocks you cannot see. Before you can find the light, my shadow of death will overtake you, ending your life on earth to be cast into the pit of everlasting darkness I have reserved for Satan and his angels.

"If you refuse to heed my warnings, then I can only cry over your pride that has led you to your destruction. My tears will be enough to fill a valley for my church whose congregations have been scattered throughout the earth. Jeremiah, say to the rulers of this country, 'Repent now of your pride and give reverence to Me or I will strip you of your positions and make you the basest of citizens. The South and the North will all fall to the enemy. All shall be removed from their homes—no one will be spared. Look now and see who is coming. The enemy is on a rampage to strip you of all your wealth. What will you do when he comes to destroy you? It is you that taught him how to overcome you. It is by your foolish actions that have led to your demise. The might you have given him has resulted in your suffering.'

"You will ask, 'Why has this happened to us?' This has come upon you because of your sins. Your iniquity is so great, it cannot be pardoned. If a leopard could remove its spots, then it could be possible for you who always practice evil to do good. You are accustomed to do evil, and so I will cast you like grain into a strong wind to be scattered throughout the earth. This is your punishment for rejecting Me by loving your lies and never honoring Me. I will strip you naked to make you ashamed, I will expose your adulteries and the abominations you have filled your lives with instead of turning to Me. How can you be made clean, America? When will you learn you cannot abandon Me?"

CHAPTER 14

There is a famine of the word of God in the land. God said, "The United States is in mourning. Its citizens' spirits are dried up by the absence of my word. Its rulers have sent out searchers to find my spirit to receive a word from Me. They languish over their sins that have caught up to them. The farmers in the field watch their fields dry up because of the dearth. Their cattle and sheep perish from a lack of direction from Me. The wild burros cannot find sustenance because of the famine in the land." I began praying, "Lord God, our sins are so many we do not deserve your mercy. Save us from your wrath. We have forgotten you were our food supply. You have been our sustenance. You have brought us the rain, your word, to meet our every need. Why have we forgotten about you? Why have we made you a stranger to us? Why have we tied your hands to make it impossible to save us? Yet, Lord, we who have our name written in the Book of Life stand in the gap for this country to forgive it for its blasphemy. We ask you to place the Holy Spirit back into this land to teach us your ways. Do not leave us without your Holy Spirit."

The Lord answered me, saying, "The people of the United States love testing out new fads. The fads are the gods they want to serve. They look for the contentment for which their flesh begs. They do not refrain from walking after their evil desires. Because they do this, I reject them and will not forget their sin. Their sin has found them out, and they must suffer the consequences. Do not pray for their deliverance. When their hearts are full of fear and they call on Me, I will not hear. When they make their confessions to Me without true repentance of their actions,

I will cover my ears. No amount of sacrifice they offer or devotions they make to Me will be considered. I will send an enemy to consume them, a famine of my word, and an epidemic of anarchy into the land."

I answered the Lord, saying, "O God, the prophets in this country say there will be no enemy to storm the land. There will be no war, only peace." God answered me, saying, "These prophets are lying. My name cannot be used to sanction the sin rampant in this country. By saying there will be no war, they are saying this nation's sins can be ignored. I have not sent these prophets. They feign these prophecies out of their own hearts. Therefore, all the prophets I have not sent who speak of peace to the United States will feel my wrath. They shall not escape my judgment. All those who rejoice in their prophecies will be cast out into the streets, losing everything. They will become food for the ravens and vultures because there will be no one around to bury them. I will pour the cup filled with my wrath upon them since their wickedness knows no end.

"My eyes are full of tears for the punishment I must pour out on this country. Its power has been broken, unable to be restored. Everywhere I walk through this land I see death and destruction. My word is not heard in the cities—everyone's spirits are broken by the absence of my word. My prophets and ministers no longer recognize this land. Its freedom and prosperity have been wiped from the earth. Have I not rejected this country as a land filled with people who have no desire to search for Me with all of their hearts? They wonder why all these evils have come upon them. They have believed there would be peace but instead found war. They sought for the healing of this land but refused to turn from their own individual sins."

I began praying to God for his mercy, saying, "God, we acknowledge our sin and all of our shortcomings. From the days of our forefathers we have sinned against you. Do not turn your back on us. Renew the covenant we made with you in the beginning. We vowed to reverence you in order to receive your blessings on our land. Is there anything the other countries can give us that you have not already given us? Those nations cannot give us rain for our crops or the sunlight to grow food. You have always been our source, and thus we will put our trust in you for all of our needs."

CHAPTER 15

God then spoke to me, saying, "Even if Moses and Samuel stood before Me, making intercession for this country, I would not be persuaded to turn away my wrath. I must cast them out of my sight. If they come to you, asking, 'Where should we go?' Answer them, those who are doomed to die to the grave, those who will be wounded by the enemy to the battle, those who face hunger to the barren fields, and those to be enslaved by the enemy to his prisons.

"There are coming four demonic spirits into this country. The first will slay the inhabitants of this nation. The second spirit will rip their possessions from them to be given to a stranger. The third will devour all of this nation's wealth, and the fourth will destroy all that is left standing. Because your president, the Congress, and the courts have abandoned Me for their own gods, I will scatter those they hope to rule to other lands, leaving them with no one to control. No nation will offer you help. None will seek your welfare. You have walked away from Me, taking steps backward and not forward. Therefore, you have given Me no choice. I am sending my judgment on you to destroy you. I am tired of allowing your sins to go unpunished. I will pass a strainer through your land to remove those who are evil from those who follow Me. Parents and children alike will all feel my wrath. This land is ripe for destruction. One city after another will fall to the enemy, all its wealth stripped away to be used by others. Terror and fear fills all of its streets, the wages of its sins too great a burden. All of its citizens it has raped all throughout the years will be removed from their control. Night has passed upon the land but not on my people. Those who escape from the cities with their possessions will be chased by my angel to strip them naked of all they carry on their backs."

I began lamenting before God, saying, "Oh, if only I had not been chosen to deliver such words of judgment to pass on to this country. I have never done anything to offend anyone. I have always tried to be pleasant to everyone, and yet now I am cursed by all who have heard my words." God answered me, saying, "It will be better for you and my people during my judgments than before they come to pass. I turn my word against the United States to punish and to purify my people. The possessions of those who have turned against Me will be taken as a spoil of war. Their sin will leave them without a home or any of their former possessions. They will be stripped bare. My anger and fury cannot be contained against them."

I began praying, "O, Lord, remember all I have suffered at the hands of those who hate the words I have spoken. Turn their words of evil against me back on them. Reward them with the evil they plan to bring on me. I have spoken the words you placed in my mouth. I have served you faithfully with your joy filling my heart. I am your servant waiting on you. I have suffered loneliness sitting among those who hate your warnings. They detest me, wanting me to be silent. Why

must I suffer so much doling out your word to those who do not want to hear? Are you treating me as one who prophesizes falsely? Where is your presence on which I have always depended?"

God replied, saying, "You have not felt my presence because you are my example. I have used you to represent this nation. If you turn from your sin, then I will restore you and bring you back into my presence. If you will remove from your hands all that offend Me, then I will bring my words of life back to you. You must not return to the evil that separated you from Me. If you want my forgiveness, then return to Me.

"Jeremiah, you are an impenetrable wall. All who fight against you cannot prevail. I will always be your defense. I will counter all their attacks against you and bring to naught all plans to silence you. I watch after my word to ensure it all comes to pass."

CHAPTER 16

God continued his word, saying to me, "Do not marry any of the women in this land. Do not produce children from those who are cursed. All the fathers, mothers, daughters, and sons in this land shall die grievous deaths. There will be no tear shed for them or graves dug for their bodies. The absence of my word in their spirits will lead to their death. The power of the enemy will trample them underfoot. I will reserve their carcasses for the dogs and the fowls to consume. Furthermore, I stress there will be no services to attend to honor those who die. There will be no one present to mourn their untimely passing. Although I wish to show them my love, I must remove my peace from them and show them no mercy. Those who rule and those who follow will not be buried. All their carcasses will be scattered throughout the land with no grave marker to identify them. There will be no pomp or ceremony to remember their names. No comforters for the dead will be found. Though one searches here and there for the body of his parents, their bodies will remain hidden, unmarked to never be honored.

"Jeremiah, you may not go into any house of those who are cursed. You will not feast with those who must shortly die. The days of celebrating are coming to an end. The days of parties, feasts, and marriages will all be cut short. After you have released all these words to this country, they will say to you, 'Why has God decided to judge us? What evil have we done? Let God name one sin we have committed.' Your answer to them shall be, 'You are being judged because of your sins. You have rejected God in your pursuit of debauchery. You have placed gods in your heart that God cannot pardon. You have turned away from God and served those idols you have set up in your lives. You have abandoned God's laws, removing them out of your sight. You have forgotten the principles your forefathers gave you, choosing to run after all the filth contained in your hearts. Your ears are dull of hearing, unable to hear God.'

"Because their sins are so many and they have rejected Me, I will remove this land's people from their homes, giving them to others. Whenever they wish, they can continue to serve those idols in their hearts. They will not receive answers to their prayers to gods that cannot help them. My Holy Spirit will not be there to comfort them. The day is coming when I will no longer be remembered as the God this country was born to seek but as the God who brought back those to this land who never turned their backs on Me.

"All my people who have been scattered by the enemy will be brought back to the homes they lost. I will seek them out so my Holy Spirit can once again minister my word to them in a time of peace. However, their spirits are not clean before Me. They are still practicing their sins. They must pay double for the iniquities hidden in their hearts. I must cleanse them of the filth that still overpowers them."

Responding to God's word I began praying, "Lord, you are my strength and my protector. You are my safe haven from the day of your wrath. The people of the nations will say, 'The United States has reaped what it has sowed. Its lies, pride, and pleasure-seeking led to its demise.'" God answered, "Can I overlook a nation who has replaced Me with money and power, as well as other idols? When my hand of judgment moves on this nation, all will know it was God who punished them for their sins."

CHAPTER 17

"The sin of the United States is carved in stone, carved in the hearts of its people where their idols rule with a rod of iron. The children observe the gods their parents serve, being enticed to join them in their sin. I will destroy the sanctuaries embedded in their hearts. I will snatch their money from them and all their goods. They will no longer be able to call the United States their home. It will be taken from them, a country they once knew no longer as it was. My fierce anger cannot be quenched against this country. It burns as a raging fire destroying all in its path.

"All people who put their trust in man and push Me away from them heap curses on themselves. They stand alone in a vast desert dying of thirst, my word of life polluted by their peers on whom they relied. All men are blessed who put their trust in Me. I am the hope of salvation, the only one who can rescue any person in this time of need. All who put their trust in Me will be like a large oak tree whose roots spread deep into the earth, firmly planted to withstand the storm. It prospers through the cold and the storm, giving its food to the animals it feeds.

"Man's heart is wicked—full of evil desires that spread like a plague to infect all those around. He cannot comprehend the depth of his corruption. I know his heart. I place tests before him to fail or pass. I reward him accordingly with my law as the standard he must be measured against. He who searches for riches hurting those in his path will die, leaving all behind to be evidence that what he gained was stolen and his life corrupt. I sit on my throne, seeing all that is happening. The spirits of all who reject Me will be cast into the earth. From Me springs the words of life. I sustain all that come to Me."

I began praying, "Heal me, Lord, of my sin. Purify my heart. I will be healed when you touch Me. I will be saved when I call on you. I offer my praises to you because you are the one who gives life. The people of this land ask me where to receive your word. They hope to hear you say your judgment is finished. As for me, I have taken no pleasure in delivering your word. Its pronouncements have weighed heavily on my soul. I obeyed you and delivered these words of destruction. I have done what is right in your eyes. I ask you, Lord, to ease this burden you have placed on me, to be a shelter for me from your wrath that comes. Cause all those who come against me to be scattered by confusion. Thwart their plans and punish them twofold. Do not let them escape your day of punishment."

God responded to me, saying, "Jeremiah, go to the Capitol and relay to this nation's rulers these words: All you government officials and all who can hear, obey my commandments. I command you to honor and serve Me. Reestablish my word back into your government halls. Restore back into this city what your forefathers placed here. They honored Me daily when this nation was young. You have forgotten Me. You have hardened your hearts against Me. You refuse to recognize your sin. If you turn from your wicked ways, then I will heal this land. I will heal these halls. I will not take this land away from you. Everything will be as it once was. You will honor and worship Me in this nation and city I founded. However, if you refuse to listen, then my judgment will be swift, destroying this city and country with a force more powerful than the sun."

CHAPTER 18

God then spoke to me, saying, "I want you to observe what happens when pottery is made. After you arrive, I will speak to you further." So I went to a place where pottery was made. A person spun a wheel to fashion a vase. However, something went wrong in the process. The man threw away the vase he had fashioned. He then proceeded to make a new vase. God then spoke to me and said, "People of the United States, am I not able to do with you as this potter has done? As this potter has fashioned this vase with his hands, you are in my hands. At any time I decide to cast away any nation who offends Me, I send my word to destroy it. If that nation will heed my warnings and turn from its sins, I will undo my pronouncements against it. At any time I speak words to build up and strengthen a nation and it then turns against Me by disobeying my laws, then I will reverse the words of blessing, sending my curses instead.

"Now, Jeremiah, go and speak for all to hear these words: To the rulers, those they oppress with their laws and anyone else living in this country, I am bringing an evil on you, a terrifying judgment. A plan is being executed at this moment to strip you all bare. To avoid my punishment you must turn from your wicked ways and begin to love your neighbor and do righteous acts. However, you have said you will continue to chase after your sins. You say, 'Because there is no hope of escaping God's judgment, we will continue to seek pleasure from every desire that fills our hearts.' Now, ask the other countries if they have ever heard of the people of the United States abandoning the God of the Bible. Could they ever have gone so far away from the God they have promoted for two hundred years? Can such a nation cut off its source of strength and independence, and still survive? Since the people of the United States and its rulers have forgotten Me and turned to the idols in their hearts to worship, forsaking the path its forefathers set them on, then there is but one reward for them. Their land shall be desecrated by foreigners. Their country shall be laid waste. All observers of my punishment on this country will be astonished. I will drive its inhabitants from their homes. The enemy will not spare as he pillages your land. I will show you my back, turning a deaf ear in the day of your calamity."

Once again I, Jeremiah, was threatened. They plotted against me, saying, "Let us seize Jeremiah and judge him by our laws. Let us get the church, the media, the academics, and all in the state and local governments to malign his character, destroy his credibility to negate the words he has been speaking." I then cried out, saying, "O Lord, hear their threats! Turn their words against them. Do I merit the fruits of evil for speaking the words you have given Me? They want to slay me, assassinate me for the good I have always meant for them. I have spoken for their benefit to stop them from chasing after their sins, which will bring your punishment on them. Therefore, God, bring your wrath down on them. Scatter their children to the four winds. Send the enemy against them to separate the wives from their husbands and the children from their parents. Increase the number of widows in the land by sending their young men into the battle. Cause your terror to fall on the land from the crying heard in every house as the enemy approaches. Do all this, Lord, because they plot to take my life. You know I have obeyed you and delivered your word, so return their iniquity back on them to receive the due punishments they deserve. Remember their sins. Mark them down in your book to record their sinful deeds."

CHAPTER 19

God began speaking to me, saying, "Get a jar and bring with you some of the rulers of this country and some of its religious leaders to the valley of Ben Hinnom outside the east gate and proclaim these words: Officials of the United States and its people, my swift destruction is coming upon you. Its suddenness and magnitude will leave you in awe. This will come upon you because of your sins, which are so many. You have turned your hearts away from Me to pursue your gods of religion, sex, power, and money. You have sought despicable practices your forefathers never dreamed would fill your society. The safeguards they put in have been circumvented by you to murder your children in the womb. Blood covers your hands, testifying of your guilt before Me. You have sacrificed your children at the altar of pleasure. Such disgusting thoughts could never enter my mind, and yet your thoughts are full of this filth, polluting your souls. Therefore, this valley you stand on will be called by a new name. Its name will be no longer known as the valley of Ben Hinnom but the valley of Holocaust. This valley represents the murder of all these children at the hands of their mothers and the hands of their abettors.

"The United States shall fall—all its wise men will give its executives disastrous advice. Death shall reign in the land, scattering bodies throughout the land to be food for the scavengers. The Capitol shall be laid waste to become a minor city in the future. Its ashes will be a reminder how power corrupts those who have never known Me. During my siege against this country, every man's hand will be against his brother. I will bring chaos into your cities to hasten their destruction. The enemy is coming to bring in my correction upon all this country's lost souls.

"Jeremiah, after you have spoken these words, break the jar you are holding for everyone to see who came with you, and tell them these words: Even as by my prophet's hand this bottle has been broken, your power will be broken, never to be restored. Your people will be scattered and your unity no more. All yours plans and schemes to increase your power will be buried, never to be dug up again. This is the future for Washington, D.C., and all its inhabitants. The enemy will sweep into the houses you bought in this city and into the offices you inhabited to purge out the remnant of the altars you built in them for pleasure. The enemy will take that which was once yours."

I returned from the valley where God had sent me and went to the people who make up his church and said to them, "God is bringing his judgment upon this country because the political and religious leaders have broken his laws and closed their ears from receiving his instruction. They have turned their hearts to stone and refuse to be corrected."

CHAPTER 20

I, Jeremiah, was placed into a jail by Pashur, a priest's son, because of the prophecies I was delivering. As was done to me, so will it be done to those who prophesize destruction to the United States. The spirit that rules in their hearts is called terror. They are terrified of the coming judgment. They want to believe no judgment will come, but God's word pierces through man's heart, dispelling all doubt.

God began speaking, saying, "You whose names are not written in the Lamb's Book of Life are going to be filled with terror of my coming judgment. You shall behold your friends and neighbors falling to the enemy. You shall watch the spirit of Nebuchadnezzar flood this land and impoverish it. Your neighbors shall lose their homes and depart, and you will be next. All the power and wealth of this country will be taken away by this spirit. You will become the basest of countries. All who attack my prophets of judgment will lose their prosperity and all they have and will die in poverty when the day of their death arrives."

I began pouring my heart out to God, saying, "Lord, I have been deceived by your words to me. Your will was too great for me, and so I spoke your words. I suffer greatly over the attacks that come against me daily. I spoke the words that you placed into my spirit that had to be born. I spoke them to my hurt because your enemies constantly reproach me to silence your words. I tried to hold back. I made up my mind to speak your words no more, but your words exploded out of my mouth, unable to be contained. I have heard the curses uttered against me. I have been aware of their plans. I know they have been waiting to catch me in my words to pounce on me and afflict me with their revenge. However,

I know you are present with me to defend me from those who want to harm me. You shall humble and impoverish them, leaving them in a state of confusion. God, you are the one who judges your people and sees into their hearts. Now, let me see your vengeance on those who wish to silence me forever. I sing praises to you, God, because you deliver those who are oppressed by the wicked.

"I curse the day I was born. Let those who announced my birth be cursed. The day it was announced that a boy was born should have been a day of mourning and not of joy. Just as the cities in the United States will receive your punishment, punish those who helped bring me into the world. I should have died in the womb or been aborted. I should have stayed in the womb, never to be born. Why was I born to see all that is coming in this country and be the one whom everyone curses?"

CHAPTER 21

The spirit of King Zedekiah sent for me, saying, "Inquire to God for us concerning the enemy who comes to conquer our land and remove us from our homes. We want to know if God will deliver us from the destruction that is fast approaching, because of God's wonderful mercy." God answered those who inquired of him, saying, "The spirit that is in you is one of appeasement. You want my mercy, but you will not confront those who wish to hang on to their sin. Do you think I am pleased with those who are lukewarm? You must choose whom you are going to serve. Because you will not give up your sins, then I will break down all your defenses. You shall not be able to overcome or withstand the spirit of Nebuchadnezzar flowing into your land. It will enter your cities and destroy them. I will also fight against you to destroy you. My anger and fury against you cannot be quelled, and so through the power in my arms I will send a plague into your cities to ravage all its inhabitants. Your capitol shall succumb, and your president and congressional leaders will fall into the hands of the enemy. The spirit of Nebuchadnezzar is already in the White House bringing this destruction. There will be no pity for the poor or for those in authority. My wrath shall bring destruction to all who live in this country.

"I set before you two paths. One path leads to life and the other to death. Whoever believes he can withstand my judgment in the city shall be visited by the sword of the enemy, the hopelessness of deliverance from his plight, and the aftermath of its destruction. All who flee the cities heeding my warnings shall live. He who stays shall lose everything. I am turning my protection away from Washington, D.C. It shall fall to the enemy who is coming. I will make it the basest of cities, removing the power from it which it once held. The president must execute true justice. He must remove the oppression he has wrought on his people, or my fury will be poured out on him. My wrath cannot be reversed if he does not turn from his wicked ways and repent. There is no hope for those who hide in the valleys or in the rocks, saying, 'No one can harm us in this place of safety. Who would dare to invade our homes?' You are not safe in these places of refuge. I will start a forest fire to burn down yours walls of protection, I will devour your assets and empty your bank accounts, destroying that idol of money you have attached to your soul."

CHAPTER 22

"Jeremiah, go again to the Capitol and utter these words to the president and the other leaders: End your oppression of the people in this country. End your campaigns against those you despise, mete out equal justice to everyone, and end the bloodbath of the innocent. If you do this, then I will not remove you from power but will restore a right spirit in this city. However, if you disobey Me, then this city shall be destroyed, and I will turn my wrath on you. I will raze it to the ground and drive out all inhabitants. I will send the enemy to lay siege on it to destroy it, bringing an end to its days as a great city. Then those in the other nations will see what has come to pass and will with astonishment say, 'Why did God do this to this great city?' The answer they will be given is, 'Because they turned their back on the God this country was founded on to worship. They chose new gods to worship and sacrificed their time to them.' Do not cry for those who died when the enemy came rushing in. Cry for those who were driven from their land who will never have the opportunity to return. All those who hope to return, whom I have driven from the land, whether he is rich or poor and a ruler or not, shall never return to this land. I will raise a wall that cannot be breached to prevent those I judge from returning. Wherever I send those I drive out will die in the place I send them.

"Those who obtain riches by stealing shall receive their due reward. When you build your houses and do not give your wages to the workman, when you deck it with rich décor to cause your neighbor to covet it, shall I not punish you for this? You strive to make yourself important and to rule others, but your forefathers were not like this. They sought equal justice for their fellow man and worked for what they earned. They were honest and prosperous because they followed my laws. Because your forefathers sought Me, they gave of their sustenance to the poor and needy. They sought justice for those who had been wronged, but your hearts and words are perverted. You claim you are the champion of the poor and needy. However, you have been corrupt, coveting what others had to make them your own. You passed your laws of violence to shed innocent blood. You sought to take from others with force through the power you had been given. Therefore, you congressmen and senators, my words come against you and your president. I am stripping you of your power. There will be no sadness over your downfall, and you will be driven from this city in shame. I will make all of your names a curse.

"Go to the towns and cities of your youth and bewail the destruction wrought upon them because of the heresy in your hearts. From your youth you have rejected Me. I gave you prosperity, and you did not reverence Me. You have said you will not listen to my words of judgment, and so the pastors you have chosen will be taken from you. The idols in your life will bring shame to your name. The wickedness you have practiced will be exposed for all to see.

"You who think you are safe in your houses of luxury will feel the tremors as the enemy nears. Like the woman about to give birth to her child, you will not be able to keep the birth of the consequences of your sin from ensnaring you. No president with all the charisma and following you desire him to have will stop my judgment from passing on to you. All of you shall be delivered into the hands of the enemy who comes. Your greatest fear is upon you. The spirit of Nebuchadnezzar is already in the land. He will lead you to your destruction and bring the enemy into your towns. I will scatter you with my winds into lands where you were not born. There you will fulfill your days, never to see your homeland again. From your president on down, I will scatter your leaders and remove them from this land. I will purge their evil from this nation to never afflict this soil again. Any ruler who brings such evil will not be allowed to prosper. I will punish him for his sins and take him off his throne."

CHAPTER 23

"Trouble is coming for my pastors who lie to my sheep to turn their hearts away from my word. You have brought division in my church to propagate your own false doctrines. You have not ministered to my lambs by feeding their spirit with my words of life. Because you have cast my word aside to fill my people with your errant doctrine, I will bring great evil upon you. I will restore those you have scattered from my church in this country and bring them back to their homes once more. I will place new pastors over them to feed them with my word and instruct them in the ways of righteousness. My people will look forward to the day when Jesus will return to earth to rule with a rod of iron that cannot be broken. He shall execute judgment and justice in the earth. He shall bring peace and prosperity to his people. Through his blood, they shall be righteous. Therefore, the day is coming when I will no longer be remembered as the God this nation sought when it was first founded, but as the God who restored his people back to this land when they fled from the enemy who purged the evil from this country."

I lamented, "My heart aches, and I am faint. I stumble like a drunk over God's words of punishment for the United States." God interjected, "Its people have filled the land with adulterers. They have divorced the God they were married to and joined their hearts to their idols. Their mouths are full of swearwords, and this nation has become desolate because of their tongues. The mountains, valleys, and forests all mourn from the evil that is abundant in the land. Therefore, there are birth pangs in this land. Nature is in discord, devastating the countryside with an uncommon number of storms. The earth reacts to the blood that has been spilled in this country, trying to force the evil out.

"My prophets and my ministers have become polluted with false doctrines. I see the evil that resides in their hearts. Therefore, I shall cause them to stumble, I will visit them with my correction. As a child must be chastened for his disobedience, my prophets and ministers shall be chastened by Me. These prophets have joined with the psychics to say there will be peace when I call for war. Their lies have led my sheep astray. They have propagated the lie that this country's people will not suffer judgment for their sin when the blood of the innocents cries from the earth to be avenged. All in this nation refuse to turn from their sin. How can a prophet who says he knows Me prophesize good times for America when unrepentant sin is rampant in the land? I will give these prophets poison to drink. Since they have polluted my words with their false doctrine, I will visit them for their deceit.

"I call on my people to ignore the prophets prophesying peace. Do not listen to their words. Their words have come out of the imagination of their own hearts. I have not sent them. I do not sanction their words. They say, 'Do not worry—these will be days of peace. There is no need to fear. There is no enemy coming.' Have these prophets been in my presence? Who has been in my midst to hear the counsel I have given?

My counsel is that there will be a powerful force of fury to strike the wicked on the head. I shall knock them over and trample them without mercy for their unrepentant sins. I will not abate my fury until all I have said have been fulfilled. I have not sent them to speak. I gave them no word, yet they prophesied in my name. If these prophets had been in my counsel and repeated the words I have said, then they would have told everyone to repent to avoid the punishment I have said will come to the United States.

"Am I not a God whose presence fills the earth? Can anyone believe I am not near and do not know what is happening in one's life? Is there anyone who can hide his sins from Me? I am near, observing everything, ready to immediately fill that need in a person's life. I am aware the false prophets have been prophesying in my name, saying I gave them a vision. How long can they continue to fool themselves? They do not recognize that these dreams of theirs have come from the unredeemable flesh in which their spirits are trapped. There is a spirit behind these visions of theirs meant to deceive my people and make them believe the lies that are being told. These prophets do not recognize the voice that is mine. Let a true prophet speak my words of truth. Let those who hear my word deliver it faithfully. The words given to my church must be tested to know which comes from Me and which comes out of a person's fleshly heart. My words break the bonds of those who are bound. It lights a fire in one's spirit. Any prophet who twists my words, uttering things I have not said will face my wrath. Cursed be the prophet who claims words came from Me when they really came from his own perverse heart. All those who entice my people into believing lies by saying they received a dream from Me shall have all their words brought to naught. I did not send them. Their words are offspring of Satan, meant to lead my people away from the truth.

"The wicked in this country and the prophets who comfort them regard obeying my commandments as burdensome. Many of my ministers look at obeying my word as impossible and to be disregarded. It has never been by works, but it has always been by my grace that people serve Me. The prophets and ministers who will keep those I want to save from finding Me and saying it is too great a burden to be borne by calling on Me will be punished. Do not deceive those among you into believing that following Me is a weight too heavy to be carried. You ministers and prophets, it is your word that is burdensome. It is your word that leads those who listen to you to their destruction. I will not permit you to pervert my word anymore. When people ask what I have been saying to you and you then reply about a burden being placed on them to obey my commandments, my fury will be poured out on you. I will turn my back on you and deliver you to the enemy. You will be cast out of your homes and your lands, never to be sought for again. I will make your name a shame to be mentioned anymore."

CHAPTER 24

The Lord gave me a vision of two baskets containing figs, representing two groups of people in the coming judgment. One basket contained ripe figs ready to be eaten, and the other basket contained figs that were spoiled. The spoiled figs had become inedible. Then God said to me, "Jeremiah, what do you see?" I said, "I see figs. There is a basket of figs that are perfect for eating, but there are also figs that cannot be eaten because they are spoiled." God then said to me, "Those people I send away from the cities, leaving their homes, I will place a marker on them to protect them in their banishment. They are being driven from their homes and land for their own good. When my judgment upon the United States is complete, I will bring them back to the homes they abandoned. I will restore that which was lost and replant them with deep roots to secure a foundation for them in which to survive. They will seek to come closer to Me and become intimate with Me. I will be their rock and provider. They shall worship Me with their whole hearts and inherit what is mine.

"The spoiled figs that have become inedible represent all those who do not heed my warnings. Everyone in the cities who do not flee in time will face my full wrath. The president and all your leaders will also feel my fury. I will scatter them among the nations, making their names a curse. The enemy shall be a scourge to chastise them. I will abandon them to their fate and hide my words from them. I will send a pestilence among them to root them out of the holes they are hiding in to escape my judgment. I will leave them no safe haven in which to hide—my angel shall uncover all their concealed places."

CHAPTER 25

God placed me as a spokesman to speak to this country during this first year the spirit of Nebuchadnezzar invaded the White House. God said, "I have given you warnings all these years to repent. I have given you signs in your weather and signs in your cities. The enemy stormed your land on September 11, 2001, but you turned a deaf ear to Me. The earth has tried to spew out the evil present in this country with fierce storms like Katrina. There are earthquakes to come and other large disasters looming. You have not hearkened to Me. I have sent my pastors and preachers to you, warning you to repent, but you still cling to your sins like glue to paper. My servants have said to you, 'Turn away from the wickedness you are practicing, so God will not visit this land and punish all of us for our sins. Rid yourselves of the idols in your hearts that pollute your souls lest you anger the God who formed you. If you do this, then God will have mercy on you and keep you from harm.' Yet after all these words of warning, you have ignored Me. You have left Me with no choice but to lift my hand of protection from you and let the curses in my word overtake you.

"Since you have not heeded my warnings, I will use the spirit of Nebuchadnezzar to afflict you. This spirit will bring the enemy into this land to destroy it. I will end your lives of leisure in this country. Your weddings, parties, and grand events will come to an end, and the sounds of mirth will no longer be heard. Your land will be full of power shortages and will be laid waste. You will become servants to those who come in to afflict this country, until I have totally purged this land of all those who pollute it. When the period of my judgment has run its full course, then I will punish those foreigners who came into the United States to destroy it. Your president will fall also, he who has succumbed to the spirit of Nebuchadnezzar. I will cause the enemy to fall in his own land, never to rise again to judge the United States. He will rise for a short time to rule many countries but will fall when it comes to the point in time I have determined to judge him. My judgment is not just for the United States, but also for those other nations that have abandoned Me for their gods of pleasure and power.

"Jeremiah, I am giving you a cup filled with my wrath to send to the nations I am determined to judge. Everyone who drinks of this cup will face my punishment. All the rulers of the United States shall be stripped of their power and their names become a curse. The rulers of Canada and its citizens will also feel my wrath. The countries in Europe, South America, Africa, and Asia will all be judged. All those who have known Me in the past and rejected Me shall not escape justice. The Arab in the desert shall not avoid my fury. I will punish those who attack my church. I will punish those who will not heed my words. You nations drink the cup of my wrath I give you. Drink to your fill and fall down in a drunken stupor. When you fall, you will rise no more. Judgment is on its way to bring you down.

"Any nation that thinks it will not drink the cup filled with my wrath will also face my fury. If I judge the United States who has sent the gospel to the world, then those other nations who have known Me will certainly not escape. Those who have been given much from Me have a greater debt to pay. I will stretch my hand over the nations to judge them. The United States is my starting point, but all the others will follow. I will bring great destruction into these other countries and many will die. I will send my angel to draw his sword and slay those I am determined to judge. From one end of the earth to the other, the dead will be scattered upon the earth. They will be food for the ravens and vultures. They will die with no one present to bury them. I am gathering a big feast for the scavengers to eat the flesh of those who took my word and rejected it. From the ruling elite to the servant, all will be judged and scattered through the earth. There will be no places of refuge to hide.

The leader and the follower will hear the wails of agony throughout the countryside as they run from the destruction overtaking them. Peace has been removed from the land—only war remains. I have lifted my hand of protection and brought down the hand of my fierce anger to destroy the nations who have forgotten Me."

CHAPTER 26

I, Jeremiah, was commanded to go before God's church and speak fearlessly to it without holding back one syllable in the hope that God's people would repent and cry out to this nation to turn from its wicked ways. God said to his church, "If you will not obey my commandments that I gave to Moses and not listen to my prophets and pastors I have sent to you, then I will abandon you to your sin and raise up another church in your place. I will do to you as I do to your cities in making you a desolate wasteland with no followers to lead. However, I know your hearts. You will not hearken to Me, and you will attack my servants who deliver this warning. You will say to them, 'Why are you prophesying such lies to us?' You will go to your political leaders and to the media to try them in the court of public opinion. You will try to silence them with your arms of flesh. One of my servants will reply, 'God sent me to deliver these words to you. I have spoken of God's coming judgment on this nation and to his silent church that have given their nod of approval for the unchecked sin rampant in this country. I am telling you to repent now before it is too late. If you repent, then God will not judge this country at this time. He will repair the breach that has opened between you and him. You can do whatever you please to me, but know I will not repent of delivering these words of warning to you. If you kill me, then you will have more innocent blood on your hands. Your blood guilt will be added to the blood already spilled by the inhabitants in this nation ensuring God's rapid reprisal.'"

God continued speaking, "In the days of Hezekiah, king of Judah, Micah prophesied against Judah, warning them of God's coming judgment, and King Hezekiah led his people in repenting for their sins. As a result of their repenting, the kingdom was delivered from the mighty Assyrians. However, King Jehoiakim killed the prophet Urijah for prophesying against Judah when Nebuchadnezzar was invading the land. He died shortly thereafter for murdering my prophet. I will not leave you guiltless for persecuting my prophets. My wrath will quickly turn on any who harm my mouthpieces of coming judgment. Know for a certainty I must cleanse this land of its evil to save those I have ordained to eternal life yet to be born.

CHAPTER 27

God said to me, "Get some wood and fashion a yoke with it and add leather straps in which to secure the yoke over your neck. After you have done this, send messages to the allied countries of the United States with this word: I formed the earth and placed man on it with the other beasts that walk the earth. I gave man dominion over the earth and made him the master over all the beasts, and now I have sent the spirit of Nebuchadnezzar into the United States to give him dominion over all its inhabitants for a time. I also place you under his dominion. All who refuse to serve this spirit who resides in the White House shall have their necks placed into the yoke by force. I will punish you simultaneously with the United States for your rebellion against Me. You will be consumed by the war, the pestilence, and the absence of my word that breaks every yoke. Therefore, do not listen to your modern-day seers who say there will be no war, and you will not be in bondage. You also shall serve this spirit of Nebuchadnezzar for a season. Whoever will heed my words and will not fight this spirit will not have its citizens scattered throughout the earth.

"I speak to the political parties in the United States opposed to the spirit of Nebuchadnezzar in the White House to end their resistance to this spirit. Place yourselves into the bondage he brings. He was elected to the office for a reason. If you resist, you will bring death and destruction upon yourselves. I have given him dominion over you and this country to bring my judgment upon it. Therefore, do not listen to those who prophesize peace and good times for America—they are speaking a lie. I did not send them to speak. They are getting you to believe a lie so that you will be scattered and removed from this land with those deceitful prophets.

"To the pastors and priests in the United States and to all others: do not believe the words of peace and prosperity for this country. Do not accept the lie of the economy recovering and becoming strong again. Bring your necks under the bondage of your king in the White House. Why should I level your cities with great destruction because of your resistance to my words? If those prophets of yours that tingle your ears speak truth, then let them intercede for you that your king will not increase his burden on you yet once more. Be aware: this spirit ruling your land will take all your prosperity and send it to other lands."

CHAPTER 28

"Do not let the prognosticators and false prophets tell you the power of the spirit of Nebuchadnezzar will be broken in the next election. I will increase its stranglehold over you. It will finish the work I have sent it to accomplish. Those who have their hearts full of evil will not return to plague this country again. I will remove them from this land, and where they go is where they shall remain. Let us have a contest to see whose words will prevail. Shall the false prophets who prophesize of my judgment being cut short before its job is finished be correct, or shall the truth be found in the prophet who says this work is a long one? To cut this work short would be to sanction the sin that exists today and let it come back to fill this land. I shall finish this work and expunge all the evil filling its borders.

"The yoke of bondage coming into this land will not be a yoke of wood but a yoke of iron. All here and in the countries allied with the king I have placed in the United States shall serve him. The elite and the poor shall all do obeisance to him. Those who resist my yoke of iron shall be judged by this new king because of their rebellion against Me."

CHAPTER 29

"Those I drive into other countries who have not abandoned Me must wait until the time my judgment is complete. This is not a short work. Build up your lives in the new lands you flee to, and wait for the day of my visitation for you. I will come to bring you home, but what must be destroyed is not a work of one day. Therefore, marry and beget children. Pray for the nations in which you now reside. Pray for peace to come to their shores and not war. It may be through your prayers, peace may come. However, false diviners will try to sway you from my word. They practice deceit to lead you to your own confusion. I have not sent them. Their dreams are false, and their visions come from within their own corrupt hearts. Run from them, and give them no heed. Their hearts are hearts of flesh and full of false doctrine.

"After a few years, I will bring you back to your homes to be restored to the land of your nativity where you will worship Me once again. I want to bring you peace and not war. I want to give you good things and not evil. When you seek Me with all your heart, you will find Me with open arms. I will heal your hearts and make the past like a distant dream. I will empty the nations to which you fled to bring you back to your homes from which you were driven. All those who will not flee from the enemy will be crushed and scattered and face my punishment for disobeying Me. I will not spare until I make a full end of them. Many shall die in the battle and in the plague that follows. My words of life will be absent to assist them in this time of need. This punishment can be avoided by this country if its people would heed my warnings and turn away from their sins.

"Those who prophesize the United States will not fall shall be delivered to the enemy for punishment. They will be treated the same as the adulterers and the murderers who are abundant in this society. They bring forth lying words I cannot abide. They concur that the sins of this country should continue without punishment. I will chastise them with a mighty hand for leading the people of the United States into a false hope of deliverance.

"Jeremiah, you and those who prophesize in my name saying this judgment is not a short one will be persecuted. They will want to nullify your words given to my followers in which you tell them to build a new life in the countries to which I drive them. Their hearts are not right with Me. They are driven by Satan to stop my judgment of purging out all the evil that has infiltrated the United States. My judgment will have a full end. I will bring those I call mine back to this country when the time of my cleansing has been fulfilled. I will punish all who come against you and deliver them to the enemy to bring my judgment on them. They shall feel my wrath for their rebellion against my word."

CHAPTER 30

"Jeremiah, I want all these words I give you published in a book. I want this published because when the day arrives when I visit my people who have been scattered to other countries, they will be able to read these words and remember the warnings I gave them before the perilous days of my judgment on the United States manifested. I want them to be able to read in the countries to which they have fled that I will return those who worship Me to the homes they were forced to leave because of the enemy.

"Now I turn my words against the people of the United States. I will bring fear and terror onto your laps. You will hear the sound of the enemy approaching, taking peace from your land. The terror you will face will draw the blood from your faces as you watch all things around you crumble. This day that is nearing will be an unparalleled day in the history of the United States. When the British had you near defeat and surrender during the Revolutionary War during those long cold winters, I was there to rescue you. I sent Thomas Paine to encourage you to continue the struggle. Now, with the fall of the United States at the brink, there will be a vacuum of my word. There will be no encouragement because it is by my design the United States shall fall. All the unrepentant sin contaminates all those who become exposed to it, and because of this, the evil in this country will be expunged.

"When I break the iron yoke placed on your necks by the spirit of Nebuchadnezzar, then this country will experience freedom again as in former days. I will bring my people back to this land, and they shall worship Me here. I will once again bring righteous leaders to govern your land that will honor Me. I will give you a fresh new start. Therefore, fear not for your future because you will be restored to this land and to the homes you will abandon. I will gather you from afar and give this nation peace instead of war. The nations to which you flee will also face my judgment, but I will always be with you to be a refuge in the storm. Because you have failed to raise your voices to save the United States from my judgment, you are being chastened by Me. Your silence is leading to the hardships you must face. I must purge out the dross in your lives to cleanse this country for a new beginning.

"The evil in this country is like an inoperable cancer. There is no remedy to save this country as it stands today. There is no nation who can help the United States. There is no salvation to be found, far or near. Its sins have increased to the point of no turning back of my judgment. Cry for mercy—it will not be heard. Only a nation who repents and turns from its wicked ways can be saved.

"My people, take heart that I will restore you back to your homes. I will bring prosperity back to this land. Those who think I cannot restore that which has been destroyed should consider Israel. They defied Me over and over and lost their land, and yet today, they are once again living in the land I promised them thousands of years ago.

When the time of your dispersal is over, I will turn my wrath on the enemy who conquered your country. I will strip them of their power and throw them out of this land. I will make them the prey and not the spoiler.

"I will bring you back to your homes, and your cities that have been laid waste will be rebuilt. Their will be joy again in the streets and praise offered to Me for my blessings. Your families shall prosper and things will be like they were before sin flooded this nation like a plague. All who oppress you will face my punishment. My blessings will once again pursue you and overtake you and frustrate those who hate you. I will give you good leaders who will be prayer warriors who will constantly seek my guidance. I will hear their prayers because their hearts will be right with Me. Once again, I will be the God of this country on whom this nation was built. Know for a certainty that this day will come after

I judge this nation for its sin, moving like a tornado through it, rooting up and destroying all in its path. My punishment on this country will not be finished until all that offends Me has been removed."

CHAPTER 31

"All the people in the restored America will be mine. Their families will be blessed and serve Me. The people of America who survive the coming storm for this nation will experience my grace in the places they flee to hide. I will cause them to rebuild what will be torn down and draw them to Me with my love. Your crops destroyed by the war will be replanted, and abundance will come from the farms once more. You will know my peace once again and will worship Me in your fields. Begin singing and shouting to Me a song of praise for the salvation I bring to those who have been tested in this time of upheaval. Bring to your lips thanksgiving for leading you out of the wilderness to go back to your homes. The rich and the poor, the healthy and the lame will return to their homeland in droves to reclaim a land they once knew as being a free country. They will come with joy and with tears while offering prayers for their families when they return. I will be their God and guide them in the path they should go so as not to stumble over the obstacles Satan will put in their way.

"I am announcing to the nations, what I have plucked up by the roots will be replanted. That which has been scattered will be herded back to these shores. I will overpower the enemy who will bring great destruction on America. Therefore, there shall be rejoicing in the cities and the fields for what I will do for America. The land will have an abundance of food once more and peace will reign in the land. All who mourn will have joy restored to their soul. All who cry will be comforted by my right hand. The pastors and priests I give you will be full of my word to fill your spirits with my living water.

"When the enemy comes, crying and wailing will be abundant in this country. However, those I bring through the storm will have their tears wiped from their eyes by my hand, and I will bring them back to the homes from which they were forced to depart. Therefore, when you run from your homes and are in a far land, remember there is hope for your children to see the land you left that they were too young to remember.

"My people will be scattered from this land and then will call on Me for deliverance. They will offer prayers of repentance for not rising up against the evil that flooded their country. I will see the shame that covers their faces and see the sincerity of their hearts. Thus I will have mercy on them in this hour of testing and chastisement. They will begin to offer prayers for the cities they had to leave, they will ask for my blessings to return to its once-beautiful shores. I see pastures full of flocks and the fields full of corn once again filling the land. I see the ground giving its abundance to feed those who have nothing and places for the weary to rest for the night in a land that once only knew discord. I am bringing sweet sleep back to your children by restoring peace to this nation and harmony in its government.

"I will guard this nation from the enemy and rebuild what will be torn down. I will correct what offends to remove the corruption before it can grow. Equality and justice will be reintroduced into the courts and the government. The intents in the Constitution will no longer be ignored. This country will know my laws once more and will honor Me as its leader. I will be the God of this country again and will wipe its sins from my memory. I am the father of this nation, I am the one who promises salvation. I will never turn my back on America if it never turns its back on Me. When I promise you good, then no man can change my mind. It is by your actions I am moved. I promise life and prosperity to my people in America, which cannot be taken away from those who continually follow Me."

CHAPTER 32

"Persecution is coming for delivering my word of judgment. The worldly church leaders, the media, and the government will all act together to silence those who say, 'Repent or feel God's wrath.' They are locked in their sin and cannot recognize they are the ones in error. The apostate church leaders will ask, 'Why are you prophesying in the name of the Lord such blasphemies? Why are you saying the spirit of Nebuchadnezzar is in the land?' Know this: the United States is being placed totally into the hands of the spirit of Nebuchadnezzar. It already controls the White House. The government of this country is being brought under total subjection to this new dictator. All of this nation's leaders will do him obeisance. This government will be completely stripped of its constitutional customs. Its laws will be ignored, ripped up, and discounted. This must continue until the time my judgment reaches its full end. Any effort to overthrow the tyranny that is coming will be frustrated and cannot prosper."

I began remembering when I was in the court of the prison how God told me my nephew would come to me to sell me his field. When Hanameel, my nephew, came to me, Hanameel said, "Buy this field of mine in Anathoth. You are the next in line according to the laws of inheritance." So I bought the field before witnesses as was the custom, and the property in the land of Benjamin became mine. I then took the proof of my purchase and gave them to Baruch, my friend. God then began speaking through me, "This purchase of the land was a representation that the Jews would return to their land and live there once again as I promised them. So will it be the same for those who will be driven from their homes in the United States. I will bring back my chosen people who will be scattered throughout the world to other countries. I will bring them back to revive a once-dead country with my spirit."

I then began praying, "God, you made the heavens and the earth. Through your mighty power, all that exists is held together by your unshakeable word. There is nothing that is impossible for you to do. You send out your love to those who will receive it and judge those who refuse your love. When they sin, you punish them according to your laws. You are an all-powerful, mighty God who is always watching the steps each man takes. Each man is rewarded according to the fruit he bears in his life. Egypt saw your mighty hand when you sent Moses to lead Israel out and led them to the land you promised them in Canaan. You blessed them in that fertile land, but they grew fat and lazy and forgot the God who gave them that land. They disobeyed you, broke your commandments, and brought the evil upon themselves, which dislodged them from their possessions. Now the United States has come to the same crossroads. You gave them this land of plenty, but they have become fat and lazy and have forgotten the God who has always been their sustenance. The enemy is coming and is already at the door. You have said this will happen and so it is coming to pass right now before my eyes. Yet, I can have hope with the purchase of this field in Anathoth that you will honor your word to your people of returning them to this country after your judgment is complete."

God then began speaking, saying, "I am the God of Adam. I created all flesh and there is nothing too difficult for Me. This country and its capitol will fall to the spirit of Nebuchadnezzar. The enemy will storm the cities of this nation and its capitol and will purge out the houses of pleasure and idol worship. They will burn your cities and empty their coffers, leaving them penniless. They will finish the work I intend to complete on this nation, because unrepentant sin is abundant in this country. I have called for this nation to repent, but it has refused to hear Me speak. I have been provoked to the point my fury can no longer be held back. Therefore, I shall remove this country from my sight and build a new one in its place. Everyone in the United States has caused my wrath to be poured out on this country. The politicians, lawyers, religious leaders, and all its inhabitants have provoked Me to bring this great distress and cleansing to this nation. I have been sending my word out to the people of this country all these decades, teaching them my principles, and meeting their needs, but it has been to no avail. Its people have turned their backs on Me to serve a god of flesh in their hearts.

"My houses of worship have been defiled by those who profess to know Me. They practice their sin in the dark and think I cannot see what is in their hearts. They condone the sacrifice of my children to Moloch, a false god who required the blood of the innocents. My apostate church does not know this is an abomination in my eyes. Blood spilled in sin satisfaction requires a penalty of blood to be repaid.

Therefore, with my silent church's nod of approval by remaining silent, I give this country over to the angel of death to kill, crush, and destroy all that I deem foul.

"After this nation is cleansed, I will cause all my people who have been chastised by Me to return to this country bringing about a new birth. I will give them peace and will be a wall of protection for them as they reestablish what was lost in a country that had forgotten its God. I will be put first again as the sovereign of this land and will place leaders in position of power here who can hear my voice. I will bring unity among the people of this country once again, which before had only known discord. I will instruct its citizens how to hear my voice and obey my commandments, so they will not stray toward the paths of destruction. I will be this nation's God, and its citizens will be my people. I give the people of the United States my promise and make a pact with them of being their protector and supplier of all their needs if they will not depart from my presence by returning to the gods they used to serve ahead of Me. I will bring my riches and joy back into this country and give its people deep roots to be anchored in this land they can always call home. Just as there will be a great measure of evil brought on the United States for its iniquity, an equal measure of good will be brought to those who come back to this land. I will restore the lands back to them whose property was taken by purchasing for them that which was stolen."

CHAPTER 33

God, bringing another word to the people in the United States, added, "I am the God who laid the foundations of the earth. Nothing is too small for Me. Come into my presence and pray before Me. I will answer your prayers. I will show you things you have not imagined or comprehended to this day. I will expose your heart and show you things to come in your life if you will open your hearts to Me. Do not be like your leaders who will resist the onslaught of the enemy invading this country. In the battle they will dig their foxholes only to have them be their graves. Their houses will be shattered and all they own will be burned by the fire. I will leave them nothing on which to put their dependence. Because of their wickedness, they resist my will. Therefore, my hand of protection will be lifted from them so they will become victims of a terrible fate.

"Peace is coming to the United States. Peace will come after the war for the nation's soul that brings my wrath. I will cure this nation of its terminal cancer. I will bring health and vitality back to these shores. I will reveal my truth to all who long to see my face. I will bring these people back to inhabit this country once more. This land will be clean from the fatal sickness that will cause its fall. I will forgive the sins of its people who call on Me as in former days. My name shall be honored before all nations for the prosperity I bring back to the United States. It will serve as a sign that a nation who puts their trust in Me will receive my blessings.

"In this country, which will be left desolate and emptied of many of its people because of my wrath, there will be life again. Though man and beast will be driven from this land and its cities destroyed, the voice of joy and gladness will return to these shores. Feasting and celebrating in this once-desolate land will return, and people will sing praises to Me for the goodness and mercy I will show them through all the trials they will have faced. Praise Me now for bringing you back to the land from which you must be driven. It is by your sacrifice of praise I can hear your petitions.

"I will restore shepherds in this land to watch over my people. In the mountains and valleys, my servants will be there. In the large cities and the small, I will feed my sheep with the richness of my word. I will bring good things to those I allow to return to this country. My blessings shall chase them down and overtake them as they set their thoughts on Me. Equal justice under the law will be practiced again in this nation because I will bring back that which was thrown out, the Constitution. Life, liberty, and freedom will once again have meaning in this land. I shall not lack a man who will seek Me with all his heart. My churches will be clean of the dirt that previously cluttered up their aisles

"If it could be possible for Me to break my word, then it could be possible for Me not to bring on you the blessings I am promising. By my word, day and night were formed. If man can end day and night that are sustained by my command, then my words could be made null and void. However, I give my promise of prosperity returning to America and peace to your land. If you can count the number of grains of sand on the beach, then you could count the number of blessings I wish to bestow on a godly nation. Do not look at the destruction I will wreak on the United States and the church within its shores, and think I will never honor my word to restore that which has been scattered to the ends of the earth. Do not believe my anger will rage forever against a people who turned their faces away from Me. If the sun and the moon could be removed out of their positions that were set there by Me, only then could the promises I am making to America be disannulled. Let it be known, those who survive the burning away of all that offends Me in America will come back to this land to serve Me once more."

CHAPTER 34

"Look now and see that the spirit of Nebuchadnezzar is already in your land. Look at the havoc it is causing. Your divisions are greater now than they have ever been. This spirit named Nebuchadnezzar will finish the work he has started on the United States. Only turning to Me and repenting for your sins can turn my wrath from you. Your cities will fall to the enemy as he rapes your land. No leader shall escape the tenacity with which the enemy will lunge at him. Nebuchadnezzar will charm him with his words and stab him in the back. Those who flee in time will leave this country, never to return.

"It is a right move to free those who are brought under tyranny, but the hearts of the leaders of America speak of such things only to deceive. They seek power to increase their importance. It is out of their selfishness they speak of being a champion of the disadvantaged. Because these leaders speak one thing and then do another, I shall bring their sins down on their heads. They have disregarded Me as important and cast Me aside for their gain. Therefore I will remove them from their positions. I will make their names a curse. All who voted for them will speak of them as dishonest and dishonorable. They will be ruined and will never rise again to power. They have lived their lives as the privileged but will end their lives in poverty. I have noticed their actions and their words and have written down their hypocrisy in my book.

"You leaders of the United States, I hold you responsible for the deceit and corruption in your hearts. You have neither hearkened to my words nor had pity on the poor. You have passed your laws in secrecy hoping no one would find you out. You feed yourselves with privileges and dole out crumbs to those who serve you. I am delivering you into the hand of the enemy. I will make you the crumbs for the birds to eat. I will take your riches and give them to others. I will make you helpless before the army that will supplant you from your seats. Washington, D.C., will be given to the enemy to plunder and destroy, never to rise again."

CHAPTER 35

I was told by God during the reign of Jehoiakim to bring the Rechabites into the temple and offer them wine to drink. So I went and brought Jaazaniah and all his kinsmen into a chamber of the Lord's house to offer them wine. I then said, "I have some wine in this chamber. Take this wine and give it to all your family and drink it." They answered me, "Jonadab, our ancestor, commanded his house to never drink wine for all generations to come or to live in the city or plant vineyards. To this day, all in this family has obeyed the commands of Jonadab, our ancestor. We have never drunk wine, lived in a city, or planted any type of crop. We have dwelt in the fields all our days. The tent has been our home. However, we came into this city to dwell because of our fear of Nebuchadnezzar and the armies he has brought into the countryside. Also, we fear the Syrians and their armies, which are near."

God then began speaking through me, saying, "Note what these sons of Jonadab did in always obeying the commands of their fathers. People of the United States, will you listen to Me like the sons of Jonadab did to their fathers? They refused to drink wine all their days, yet I have been speaking to you generation after generation only to see your ears were too stopped up to listen to Me. I have sent my pastors, priests, prophets, and others constantly warning you to turn from your sins or face my judgment. I have warned you to stop worshipping those idols in your life, but have you heard anything I have said? No, you have turned your back on Me, saying, 'We will worship the gods in our hearts who give us pleasure. We will not serve a God who will remind us of our sin.' Since you have turned a deaf ear toward Me and have declared in your hearts you will continue in your sins, then I will fulfill all the things I have said will happen to you for rejecting Me. I have spoken to you clearly, yet you have refused to hear my voice. I sent you my messages, and yet you never answered Me. Because of the deafness of your ears and the tongue you are unable to loosen, I will allow the enemy to come in and punish you for your sins. I will not be a shield to you in your day of distress—however, I will be a comforter and help to those who do hear my voice and call on Me."

CHAPTER 36

In the fourth year of the reign of Jehoiakim, king of Judah, God began speaking to me, saying, "Write down all the words I have given you concerning Israel, Judah, and the other nations from the days of Josiah until now and put them in a book." I, Jeremiah, did as I was commanded and today God is speaking to me to republish these words. God said, "Jeremiah, rewrite the words I gave you and apply them to the United States concerning the judgment to come and the judgment that will be passed on to other nations who defy Me. It might be possible the people of the United States will fear that all I say will come upon them if they do not turn from their wicked ways and repent. If the people in the United States will repent of their sins, then I will hear their voices and forgive them of all their iniquities."

So I set out to rewrite all my words of the past for the United States, and all who read these words can see it has now been accomplished. The words in this book are for all people in the United States and especially for those in his church. God said in 2 Chronicles 7:14, "If my people, who are called by my name, shall humble themselves, and pray, and seek my face, and turn from their wicked ways; then I will hear from heaven, and will forgive their sin, and will heal their land." God calls on his church to repent now before it is too late to withhold his judgment. This is your last warning before his fury will be poured out on every inhabitant in this country. It is possible to avoid the destruction that is coming if everyone will hear these words and turn away from the evil they are practicing. Your youth are exposed to the evil that fills your lives and thus taints their souls. Repent today, or God will bring to pass all the words of judgment he has pronounced against this country.

Baruch took the scroll he had written containing my words of warning and read them aloud for all to hear in the Lord's temple. Then Michaiah told the princes what words he had heard from my book, and they asked Jehudi to bring Baruch to them. So Jehudi fetched Baruch, and he came and read my words before all the princes. When the princes heard these words, they became frightened and told Baruch they would inform the king of all the words they had heard. They then asked Baruch, "How did Jeremiah give you these words?" Baruch answered them, "I was sitting in front of Jeremiah and wrote down all that he said with ink in this book." The princes then said to him, "Go and hide with Jeremiah to a location you cannot be found. Do not let anyone know where you will be hiding." Then the princes went to the king and told him all that I had said in the book. The king then told Jehudi to bring the scroll containing my words and to read what was written therein to him. When Jehudi read these words to the king, the king took each leaf that had been read and cut them up and cast them into the fire. No one became upset over what King Jehoiakim had done. Only Elnathan, Delaiah, and Gemariah asked the king to not burn the scroll, but Jehoiakim ignored them. Then the king told his people to arrest Baruch and me but God protected us from being found.

God said, "Just as King Jehoiakim destroyed the scroll with the words I gave Jeremiah, the spirit of Nebuchadnezzar will cut up and ignore the Constitution of the United States. This spirit will enslave this country and bring his wrath against my church to stop my word of judgment from coming to pass. However, my word cannot be suppressed or halted. All the words I have pronounced against the United States will be fulfilled containing my wrath. King Jehoiakim thought he could negate my words by throwing them in the fire, but I countered his actions by telling Jeremiah to publish again what he had destroyed and add extra words I would give him. Nebuchadnezzar will try to stop my word through control of the press and all forms of media, but just as I protected Jeremiah and Baruch, I will thwart every attempt he makes to stifle my word. I will punish those who attack my prophets who prophesize of my judgments coming on the United States. I will not spare but will add more punishments to those in authority. They have blasphemed my name to the other nations by practicing their witchcraft. I will not look the other way any longer. You cast my principles aside contained in the Constitution and castigate my pastors who speak against your whoredom. I shall not let the sin of the leaders in this country escape my judgment."

CHAPTER 37

God spoke to the appeasers, saying, "Those who seek to call on Me without giving up the idols in their hearts will be judged. When you call for mercy from Me for the United States, you will not be heard. Do you think I can abide the sin rampant in your country to continue like a spreading cancer by simply answering prayers for mercy without repentance? Do you not know you cannot compromise with sin? Just as I had to clean out the unrighteous in Canaan to give Israel their promised land, I must clean out the unrighteous in this country to give the United States a new beginning. It cannot stand when evil rules the land. The earth will vomit out nations that only practice evil.

"Do not look to the Canadians for deliverance, they cannot help themselves. Do not look for Europe for assistance, they have been blind for a season. Look to Me for help. I am the way, the truth, and the life. All who call on my Son shall receive salvation. Since you do not offer Me that which I require, I am delivering the United States into the hands of the enemy. The enemy is like a train that cannot be stopped. Although you fight against the enemy in the political realm, it is as an empty gesture. I require true repentance from the heart to stop this enemy. He is mighty and merciless and my chosen one to tread you under his feet.

"My prophets who pronounce my coming judgment on the United States shall be persecuted. Some will be arrested and some will be harmed. All will face the wrath of the unrighteous that have no fear of Me. Nevertheless, I loosen the law of sowing and reaping on those who attack my prophets. He who strikes my child shall also be struck. He who kills one of my own shall also face death. Pray that your children will not reap the curses you bring on yourselves for attacking my sons and daughters who defend my words.

"The appeasers in this country will come to my prophets asking for a word from God, hoping to hear my judgment will not finish its work. I tell those who have the spirit of Zedekiah operating in their lives that they will not escape my punishment. They have allowed the evil to go on in this country, including the attacks against my church, while hoping their prayers to Me would be enough for them to escape my wrath. I speak to you who have Zedekiah's spirit inside of you: you will face my judgment. I warned you to turn from your sins or else your land would be judged, but you have never listened. Turn to those who told you good times are coming to the United States and seek their help. They are the ones on whom you have always placed your dependence. Put your trust in them. Can any man deliver himself from my wrath? Ignore my words and put your trust in your riches and let us see whose words will stand."

CHAPTER 38

"The day is coming when all those who speak against what is happening in the United States will be in constant peril. There will be plots to arrest them and also to kill them. Those who preach that my judgment is coming will say, 'Flee from your homes now. The enemy is coming to take all you have and to destroy you. With him come destruction and horrible diseases to afflict all who stay to hide in their sin. Your cities are given to a people whose language you do not understand and to take their wealth for someone else to squander.' Although the people of the United States have so many sins that they cannot be numbered, they will add to their sins by going after those who call on this nation to repent. These people will say, 'These preachers are weakening the resolve of our leaders to solve the problems in this country. There is a separation of church and state, and thus these people should be punished for interfering in our affairs.' He who can understand, know what is happening. Those who succumb to the spirit of Zedekiah, who have a little sympathy for Me, who reside in the government will give in to these calls for persecution against my church. They will take my people who speak out against the government and will cast them into prisons to try to silence their voices.

"Jeremiah was cast into prison by Zedekiah and his princes because they said, 'This man should be executed, he is weakening us internally to withstand the enemy. The defenders on the walls are frightened by his words and losing their will to fight. All the words he speaks are meant to harm us.' The words of this tenor will be repeated again to arrest and imprison my people who call on this nation to repent, but as I did for

Jeremiah and Peter, I will do for those who obey my voice. I will be with them to deliver them from my adversaries. Ebedmelech pleaded to Zedekiah to remove Jeremiah from the dungeon where he would soon die, and Zedekiah listened to him. Jeremiah was removed from the dungeon to the court prison. My people who are harmed will also receive my deliverance. Although many seek their life, I shall give them some deliverance for what they must face. They must go through a trial of fire to be cleansed of the filth that has polluted their souls in this country.

"Just as Zedekiah went back to Jeremiah to ask him for another word from Me in hope I would reverse my words of judgment, those who have his spirit will seek words from Me again in hope this nation's sins will not be punished. Do not worry, my servants, who speak the words I command you to speak. Yes, they will put you in their jails, harass your families, and steal from you, but I will always be with you to deliver you. This will be a time of fire this country has never known. You must suffer just as my prophets of old suffered. I am the deliverer, I am the healer. I am healing this land from the desecrators of my word. Know that in this hour of need, you are the light that shines to rescue those lost in the dark. You will watch the horror of what befalls the inhabitants of this country and watch your fellow brothers be scattered throughout the nations. I will empty this nation to throw out the trash and bring back those of my new church who will have been cleansed by my righteous fire.

"Jeremiah pleaded for his life before Zedekiah and he hearkened to his plea. Plea to Me for your deliverance from the trials you will face, and I will lighten the load you must bear. I am always standing without listening for your voice, so I can enter into your heart and rapidly meet your needs. Those in the government who seek your harm will only have power over you for a short time before my wrath makes a full end of them."

CHAPTER 39

God began speaking to the people of the United States, saying, "When the time of my judgment visited Zedekiah and the kingdom of Judah, they were not ready. I have pleaded with you and pleaded with you to end your sin, but you have not listened to my words. Zedekiah waited until it was too late to flee, and he was captured. This will be the fate of all those with his spirit who know Me a little but will not give up their sin. You will wait for the enemy to come to your door to take what you have left, even the bottle from your baby, which your child shall see no more.

"The spirit of Nebuchadnezzar has already begun his siege on this country. He will bring in the forces to complete the task he is predestined to fulfill. Your cities will be plundered in the siege to remove their wealth and resources, and their water supplies will be shut off to hasten their fall. I give to Nebuchadnezzar his heart's desire for power, but it will only be for a season after he has wrested the United States from the sinners overwhelming this country. The poor of the land will be left to roam the empty cities and towns observing the devastation the enemy will wreak on this land. Those servants of mine left in the jails for speaking my words will win their freedom again after my judgment is past. My children, do not fear the enemy who is coming to conquer this land. He is your savior to release you from the hand of Satan, who has led the people of the United States into unspeakable debaucheries that cannot be allowed to continue. I am the way, the truth, and the life. Turn to Me for your salvation from the enemy who is too powerful for you to overcome. His power will be short-lived, and then I will bring you back to your homes to a new land wiped clean of the sin once prevalent in your land."

CHAPTER 40

Jeremiah was released from the prison after the Chaldeans had taken Jerusalem and was told he would be allowed to stay in the land of Judah or wherever he chose to go. Nebuzaradan, the captain of the Chaldean guard, said to Jeremiah, "The Lord your God pronounced all this evil on your nation because it failed to heed his warnings and continued in its rebellion against his commandments, therefore this land has become desolate. Now, I give you a choice: you are free to come with me to Babylon where I will look after you, or you can stay here and go wherever you wish." Jeremiah decided to stay in Judah at Mizpah where Gedaliah was made governor. Others who came to Mizpah were Ishmael, Johanan, Jonathan, and Seraiah. Gedaliah told them all to obey and serve the Chaldeans so things would go well for them in the land. However, there was a conspiracy about to unfold. Johanan warned Gedaliah that Ishmael had been sent by Baalis, the king of Ammon, to kill him. Gedaliah refused to believe this. He said, "Do not say such things about Ishmael. He is my friend and would never do such a thing. All that you are saying about him is a lie."

God said, "Just as there was a conspiracy to fight against the Chaldeans who had conquered the land of Judah, there will be a conspiracy to overthrow the enemy that will control the United States. Is this wrong? It is by my hand that all the evil I have pronounced will come on the United States. I will bring them into power, and I will remove them by my power. It will not be by an arm of flesh they will be removed but by the power of my spirit. I will set in motion events that will cause their fall. Do not go against that which I have decreed. If unrepentant sin is in your hearts, then all your efforts will be for naught. You will face the judgment reserved for those who do not repent of their sin. I will not allow you to stay and pollute this nation I will rebuild. Repent of your sins and live, and then you can stay in the land and serve Me. Many of my people will be driven from this land, but I will bring them back to be a blessing to this land, which before was filled with blood. I will not help those whose hearts are full of pride. I will send you away to another land to spend your last days and perish."

CHAPTER 41

A few weeks had passed when Ishmael with ten other men came to Gedaliah and feasted with him. Then Ishmael arose with his followers and killed Gedaliah just as Gedaliah had been warned would happen. Upon killing Gedaliah, the eleven men began slaying all who served Gedaliah and the Chaldeans who were in the city. After two more days, eighty men from Shechem, Shiloh, and Samaria came to make offerings at the Lord's house that had rent their clothes and cut themselves to show their remorse over all that had happened to the land. Ishmael went to meet them, pretending to be in mourning and asking them if they came to see Gedaliah. He led them into the city, killed them, and then threw their bodies into a pit. However, ten men did plead for their lives, offering Ishmael treasures of wheat, barley, oil, and honey. So Ishmael spared their lives to take what was theirs. After Ishmael had done all this, he then added to his sin by carrying away captive all that remained of the people in Mizpah, including the king's daughters.

God said, "See what the motivation of Ishmael was. His heart was not to fight the enemy that had conquered the land but to be rewarded with material things. Those who will fight the enemy who conquers the United States I have not spoken to will also be fighting for material things. You whose heart is not right with Me will be functioning out of the carnal desires that fill your hearts. Your thoughts and intentions are an abomination to Me. I will not let you stay in this country to pollute this land again that I am wiping clean of its sin."

Johanan, who had warned Gedaliah of Ishmael's intentions, then gathered men to go after Ishmael. Johanan's forces then caught up with

Ishmael in Gibeon, upon which the people Ishmael had taken captive rejoiced and ran toward Johanan's company. Ishmael, who knew he could not defeat Johanan, fled to Ammon with eight of his men. Johanan then took all these people he had collected and went to Chimham to prepare the people for a journey into Egypt.

God said, "Johanan was doing what was right in his eyes, but yet his heart was not right with Me. He had not spent his life seeking Me and learning to hear my voice. He acted like the vast majority of Americans, responding to the stimuli in his surroundings and situation. He had a conscience of what was right but a tin ear to hear my direction. My church in the United States is full of people like Johanan. They have an idea what is right and act out of their conscience, but because of not spending time to learn of Me and to hear my voice, they have no concept of what my true will is for their situations. They will fight the enemy in this country using methods conceived from their fleshly hearts but will not find the direction I want them to go. All that will befall the United States is at my command. Those in my church who do not seek Me until they find Me will only fall to the enemy and face my coming wrath against this land. I call on my people in the churches throughout the United States to purify their hearts, turn from their sins with true repentance, so I can heal this land and stop the enemy who seeks their nation's destruction."

CHAPTER 42

Johanan, his captains, and all the rest of the people from the least of them to the greatest came to Jeremiah and said, "Pray for us before God to hear our prayer and show us what to do next. We are but a few people and need his guidance." Jeremiah answered them, saying, "I will go before God and pray for you and will give you his answer. I will not hold back one word he gives me for you." They then answered Jeremiah, saying, "Let God be our witness that we will do whatever the Lord commands us to do through his word to you. It does not matter if it is a good thing or a bad thing, we will obey God's command. We want his guidance so all will go well with us."

After ten days had passed, Johanan and all his forces with the people were informed to come to Jeremiah to hear God's word for them. When all the people were gathered together, Jeremiah said to them, "God has given his word and he says, 'If you will not flee into Egypt but stay in this land I have given you, then I will rebuild you into a nation again and not tear you down. I will replant you into this land and not pull you out by the roots because my wrath against you has been sated. Do not fear any retribution by the king of Babylon from whom you are fleeing, because I am a shield and will protect you. I will give you my mercy and return you to your land. However, if you will not listen to Me and decide you will flee into Egypt to escape Nebuchadnezzar's hand, then the sword you fear will overtake you in that land. The famine also will follow behind his army, and it is in the land of Egypt you will die. This will be the fate of all men who flee into Egypt. The sword, famine, and pestilence shall bring my fury on all who go into Egypt. Just as I destroyed Jerusalem because all its inhabitants were in rebellion against Me, I will do the same to those who flee into Egypt. If you go into Egypt where I have forbidden you to go, then you will die there and see this land no more.'" Jeremiah added, "God has told you not to return into Egypt where your fathers once abided. However, I know that it is in your hearts to not heed the words God has spoken, but you will flee into the land of Egypt. Be aware, therefore, you will die in Egypt by the sword and pestilence."

God said, "The words I gave Jeremiah then stand today. If you will not get your heart right today and will not obey my commands, then fleeing into Canada or any other country will not save you from my wrath. I will consume you in any country to which you flee. That which will happen to the United States will happen in other countries. I will bring the spirit of Nebuchadnezzar with all his allied forces into these other rebellious countries and judge them also. The United States is the first of my targets because to it I have given the most. It has been the most blessed of all nations. It was brought into being by a people who sought my words and worshipped Me. It has been the country from where my gospel had been spread to the rest of the world. Now it will be destroyed and its people scattered. Those whose hearts are dark will have my destroying angel follow them into the lands they go. None of them shall return to this land to pollute it anymore."

CHAPTER 43

After Jeremiah had finished delivering God's words to the remnant of the Jews fleeing from Nebuchadnezzar, Azariah, Johanan, and all the men full of pride answered Jeremiah, saying, "All that you have said is a lie. God did not tell you to say to us that we should not flee into Egypt. Baruch, who is the son of Neriah, has put you up to this to lie to us so we will fall into Nebuchadnezzar's hand. You want the Chaldeans to kill us and take some of us into captivity to be their slaves in the land of Babylon." Thus, the remnant of the Jews under the leadership of Johanan and his captains refused to obey God's commands. Upon which Johanan and his captains took all the people they brought with them including Jeremiah into Egypt, arriving in the city of Tahpanhes.

Then God began speaking to Jeremiah, saying, "Take some large stones and hide them in the brick kiln located at the pharaoh's house in this city in front of all the Jews, and give them my word." So Jeremiah took some large stones and did as he was commanded and said to the people of Judah, "God says, 'I will bring Nebuchadnezzar, my appointed one, into this city to set his throne on these stones I have hidden. He shall set up his court here. When he comes, he will afflict the land of Egypt, bringing death to those appointed to die and captivity to those appointed to serve the Chaldeans. The gods of Egypt will be burned by Nebuchadnezzar, and all will be given to him to do as he wishes. The land of Egypt will be crushed by his might, and he shall return to his land in peace. All the idols of the Egyptians and your gods will be burned in the fire.'"

God said, "The people of the United States have the same heart as this remnant of the Jews who fled to Egypt. They do not have an ear to hear my voice or the desire to serve Me. They are trapped in their sins to this day, serving gods like money, sex, and power in defiance of my commandment of not placing any god into their lives ahead of Me. People of the United States, because you serve your false gods and refuse to turn from the idols in your hearts, your gods will be burned. I will place you into a destructive fire that will destroy your lives and give you over to an enemy you cannot overcome. Your fate is sure and cannot be altered because you have chosen to serve the evil desires that fill your hearts. I will not turn away from bringing on you all the evil I have promised will come upon you the day of my judgment. You will be removed from the homes you have, to flee into a land that is not yours, where you will die, never to return to the homes you once knew."

CHAPTER 44

God began speaking to me again, saying, "To those Americans who I will remove from their homes, causing them to flee from the enemy, you will see my judgment upon America including the devastation I bring upon its cities. Your cities will become barren wastelands devoid of its former inhabitants except for the very poor. All this devastation will occur because of the gods you serve in your hearts whom your forefathers never knew. Your wickedness is a stench in my nostrils and must be judged. I have sent you pastors, teachers, and prophets to warn you to turn from your sins, but you have refused to listen. Therefore, my fury will be poured out on you in the cities in which you dwell to drive you out of them and out of the country you once called home. I will remove the evil from this land you pollute with your wickedness by driving you far away from here, never to return.

"Why do you insist on never ceasing the sin that fills your hearts, so that my judgment will come on this country? Why do you want Me to bring such devastation on it, so no one will be left to enjoy the fruits of the labors that brought this nation so much prosperity? You have provoked Me to the point where I have to make you a curse and an example to the world of what happens to a country that turns its back on Me.

"Even in your banishment in the countries I send you, you will not turn from your wicked ways. You will continue to serve the gods in your hearts and will not consider that the devastation I will bring upon the United States will be because of the evil that is now rampant in this nation. You will not humble yourselves before Me or obey the laws I placed in your hearts when you were born. Therefore, I will chase you from your land and pursue you to the ends of the earth, bringing my curses upon you. The enemy and the destruction from which you flee will overtake you in the lands to where you wish to escape. Canada will be no refuge—it must face my wrath. I will search for you and send the dogs after you to uncover the places you seek to hide. Poverty and pestilence will always be nipping at your feet to keep you in peril and not allow you to return to this country anymore.

"You will defy Me in the lands to which you flee, saying, 'We will not serve a God who punishes us for our sins. We refuse to listen to words of coming judgment. We wish to continue to live the lives of pleasure that our hearts enjoy. We will continue to honor that which we deem is important. Before the enemy came into the land, all was going well for us. What happened in the United States had nothing to do with God's judgment. We wish to rebuild our lives and make them as they were before because that is what made our lives enjoyable. We will never serve a God who requires us to abandon the desires that fill our hearts.'

"I say to you that I have observed all the evil you have done all your days. Do you really think I could never have noticed? Because you have filled this country with your sins, you have left Me no choice but to destroy it and start over again, building a new nation in its place. Your land will become desolate, devoid of its people, and the other nations will stand in awe of the power that will bring about its collapse. It is because of the unrepentant wickedness in the United States I must squeeze it through the winepress of my wrath."

God added, "You will continue your defiance toward Me by saying, 'We will not end satisfying our souls by feeding them with that which we desire in our hearts. We vow to worship the ones who will satisfy our needs.' Since you will declare in your hearts you will never abandon your sins, I will remove my presence from you wherever you reside and leave you to your fate. With the lifting of my presence, my judgment will fall on you and overtake you. You will be consumed by my wrath with no mercy coming from Me to assist you in your real time of need. I will continue my judgment on you until no one is left to pollute this nation anymore. Let us have a match and see whose words are stronger. Call out to the gods in your hearts, and see if they can enable you to overcome my words and bring you back to this country to live the lives of sin to which you have become so accustomed. I will give you a sign to show you my words ring true and you cannot escape my wrath. I will also visit my wrath on the nations where you hope to flee. This includes Canada, who will succumb to the power of the enemy that is coming to destroy the United States."

CHAPTER 45

God now turned to his people in the church, saying, "Do not worry about the judgment that is being passed on to the United States. I know it is a fearful thing to see my wrath poured out onto a nation. I know you are worrying about your future and where you will go. Do not let any of these things enter your minds. I am coming to give you peace and assurance about what lies ahead in your futures.

"That which befalls the United States must come to pass. What I have raised up must be torn down. That which I have planted must be rooted up. The United States must be cleansed of all that is in it which offends Me. I will give you the things you need and give you the directions you desire to go. What I have placed in your hearts must be manifested. Do not look to the material things you have become attached to in the United States and desire them anymore. They were temporal and have led you astray in seeking a deeper relationship with Me. Seek Me always, and I will be a shield to you wherever I send you in the world. I will punish any person or nation that tries to harm my people. Therefore, turn your attention toward Me and all will go well with you."

CHAPTER 46

God began bringing his word against the other nations who will face his punishment. God said to Canada, "Alas, Canada, you are not prepared for the battle that is fast approaching your shores. You need to get ready for the army coming to your doors. The time of your judgment is upon you. Your defenses will be shattered and your people will be struck with fear by the power of an enemy you cannot withstand. Why is this coming upon you? You have turned your back on Me to sate the evil in your hearts. You attack my ministers who deliver my words. You arrest those who speak out against your crimes against Me. You shall feel my wrath for abandoning Me.

"None of you will be able to escape my wrath. I shall drive you backwards until you have no place left to retreat. You are as an Egypt, where people flee to escape from their pursuers, but your Nebuchadnezzar is coming to make your land a desolate wasteland. In your pride you will say, 'I will be victorious over the enemy. I will drive him back and cast him from my land.' However, your defenses are useless against this Nebuchadnezzar. I will fight for him to defeat you and your pride to bring an end to your arrogance. The nations on whom you depend will not be able to rescue you on the day of your fall. My wrath shall come on them also who have turned their backs on Me.

"The enemy will come into your land like a flood to overwhelm you and will make himself drunk with your blood. You will be like an evening sacrifice whose life must be cut short when darkness begins to fall. I have made a search for any medicine that would heal your disease, but alas, there is no cure for the wickedness residing in your hearts. As the enemy sweeps through your land taking all you possess, the nations will hear the cries of your citizens weeping over your fate. I will drive your citizens out of their homes and make them servants to a new master who will not spare anyone who gets into his way. Those who flee to your country from the United States will seek to flee to another land because my judgment will overtake them as they try to escape my wrath.

"I am bringing down my wrath on the government of this land. They have passed their laws to eradicate Me from its people's lives. I will not spare you for the wickedness in your hearts. I will bring this government down to serve another lord. Moreover, I am bringing desolation to your cities by driving out all their inhabitants. I will do all this to you because you have rejected my word and the principles I gave you. Once, you were beautiful in appearance, but now you are filthy and corrupt. All those who were attracted to you will abandon you to your fate. They shall flee to escape my wrath that overcomes you on the day of my visitation. The enemy is preparing to lay siege against your country. He is cutting down your forests for the wood to build the bulwarks for the siege. His work will not be complete until your nation falls. However, after my judgment has passed, Canada will be restored.

"To my people who flee into Canada, do not fear the sword of the enemy coming into this nation. I will keep you safe and bring you back to your homes when the time of your visitation arrives. I am your rest in the places you reside, so do not fear what must come to pass against all nations I am judging for turning away from Me. You are being corrected and cleansed from the sins that have tainted your souls, so rest in Me—I will make you whole."

CHAPTER 47

God turned his words of judgment against the Palestinians in Gaza and elsewhere, saying, "A flood of my wrath is coming against you, Palestinians, because of your hatred of my people. You have filled your land with violence and impoverished those among you to satisfy a bloodlust against my chosen ones. You seek to create many widows in Israel, but instead there shall be weeping across your land. I am sending an army to you with the rumbling noises of tanks to make your fathers flee for their lives and leave their children behind.

"The day of your destruction is rapidly approaching because of the old hatred inside your hearts. I am sending an army to spoil your land and divide you even more. Gaza will be made bald and all its inhabitants scattered throughout your borders to make you easy prey for the enemy who is coming to break your power once more. How long must my sword be used to punish my adversaries? It cannot cease as long as the Palestinians continue their violence against my people."

CHAPTER 48

God brought his word against England, saying, "Alas, to the country whose empire spread around the world, the day of your visitation has arrived. Your cities are destroyed and have become desolate because you abandoned Me for your gods of pleasure. Your power has been stripped from you and your empire is no more. The enemy has made plans for you and is coming to cut you down. The weapons he has formed will pursue you and bring great destruction. Your children are weeping and your families are all in distress for the wave of violence entering your land. From Birmingham to London, you all must flee—run into your countryside to escape my coming wrath.

"Your day is upon you because you did not put your trust in Me. You have left Me to serve your idols by placing them in your hearts. I will destroy these gods of yours and take you into captivity for abandoning the one who brought you life. No city in your nation shall escape my approaching wrath—the valley and the plain will also be destroyed. I will make your cities desolate, emptying them of people, and bring my curses upon you to chase you wherever you go.

"England has been living a life of ease since its youth and has become fat with its success. It has withstood the attack of nations and let its pride soar. Therefore, because you have become fat and forgotten the God who formed you and protected you from all your enemies, I will cause you to become wanderers in your own land, seeking a place to hide. I will once and for all break your pride that has separated you from Me.

"How can you in your pride say you are a mighty and powerful nation when your words are being turned against you by the power of my hand? I am sending the nations to spoil you and strip you of your young men. Your day of calamity is fast approaching and can never be withstood. I call on the nations around the world to lament the day of England's passing, and I can hear them asking, 'How could such a nation like this give up its strength and fall?'

"The spoiler is entering your cities with a desire for all your possessions, and your citizens are fleeing to escape the massacre that is sweeping across your land. You are destroyed, England, your pride has let you down. My judgment has come upon you to spoil all that make up your nation. London, Birmingham, Leeds, Liverpool, and all your cities will feel my judging hand. You cannot escape what I am bringing upon your country. I am breaking your source of power and removing all your wealth so you cannot stand before an enemy and continue to express your defiance.

"England has put itself above Me in its thoughts and no longer honors my word. For all these sins, I am going to bring confusion into this nation. You have spoken against Israel and tried to compromise their protection, and because of this, I am acting against you to protect my chosen ones. Oh, inhabitants of England, you must flee from your cities before it is too late. Hide under rocks and in caves to escape the enemy racing into your countryside. The pride and arrogance of England is famous among the nations, but all this pride and arrogance cannot save you from my hand.

"I see all your wealth and abundance being removed by the spoiler, and I also see all joy and gladness being absent from your country. Cry and wail for the destruction of your cities, because they are all desolate and poor. The enemy has crushed them and emptied them of all the treasures within them. Your gods will fall before Me including your god of money, and I will burn them in the fire to cleanse this country from all things stored in your hearts. You shall mourn day and night over the losses you must bear, but all of this will come upon you because you left the one you once worshipped for false gods who cannot hear.

"I hear lamentation and weeping for this country and confusion abundant everywhere as people keep on asking how a once-powerful nation could fall so quickly and easily. I have spoken: the enemy is coming into this land to destroy your pride and power. You will flee from him in terror and fall into his traps as you experience what it means to feel my hot wrath. All of you in this nation will face the cleansing fire which will devour all things that have filled your hearts that offend Me. Your children shall be taken from you to be servants to your enemies. However, after my judgment has passed upon you, I will restore your land back to you and give you a new beginning."

CHAPTER 49

Concerning the European Union, God said, "Why have you forgotten about Me? Why have you cast Me aside? I once was the God you worshipped but am now thrown away like your trash. Because you have turned away from Me and cast Me out of your sight, I am going to visit you with my destruction and send fire into all your cities. I will punish all your governors and take them out of their seats to clean out the old and bring in the new who will honor Me once more. You removed Me from my throne and placed your idol of money there instead. In addition, you have added to your sin by killing the young and old for your convenience. Why do you put your trust in wealth that decays, grows old, and perishes? Look and see what I will bring upon you for your rejection of Me. I am bringing fear upon all your people who feel this terror rushing in toward them from all sides. Your people will run in every direction to try and escape the captivity I am placing on them. However, when I finish my wrath upon you, I will bring you freedom again."

Concerning Russia, God said, "Why are you so foolish? Do you not have any wise men? Why has wisdom become a commodity that can no longer be bought? I am bringing a day of trouble upon you that will quickly destroy your land. You have lived your lives in secret and held these secrets close to your hearts, but you cannot hide them anymore because I will expose them all for the world to see.

"You think you will not face my judgment because you are far away, but why would I punish others and let all your sins go on as if they were for free? Those who call on Me will fall under my protection, but you who deny I exist shall feel the weight of my judgment. I swear on my name that Moscow and your other cities shall be laid waste and made desolate. The sound of an enemy is being heard in the distance that is coming to destroy your nation. The enemy will not stop and will crush you into insignificance.

"You have always been proud of the power you have produced, you have always felt you were safe with the large extent of your land. However, it is your pride that is leading you to a swift fall. I am coming against you to bring that high pride down. Your land is going to become a desolate wasteland. The nations of the world will be astonished at the destruction to be wreaked on you. Many of your cities of refuge will be destroyed, never to be inhabited again, because of your pride and the worldliness in your hearts. The enemy that storms your land is too powerful for you. Who do you have fighting for you that can withstand the army for which I fight? You will fight against my army, but you will never be able to prevail. I am sending an enemy to ravage your countryside and take all you have. I will broadcast to the world the details of your fall and lay out all your sins. Cry and howl for Russia, it has met its bitter end."

Concerning Syria, God said, "There is a sound of an evil omen being heard in the city of Damascus. It has become afraid and is looking where to flee. How has the city that once was the city of my joy become spoiled? Its young men will fall in its streets as its army is crushed by the enemy coming to destroy it for its hatred of all those I call dear. I will destroy its palaces that house its leadership. I will send a fire to consume all of Damascus. I am bringing an end to that line of men who hate my precious chosen ones."

Concerning the Arabs, "I have prepared the Muslim brotherhood to feel my wrath for rejecting Me. Your hatred for all your fellow man has reached the point where I must act. I will spoil your tents and bring you down until you know who it is that sits on high. Run away while you can, because fear is coming in to bring terror into your hearts. The servant I have chosen is making his plans to tear your kingdoms down. Flee to the nations who are at ease to escape my punishment. He will enter your lands to scatter you to all parts of the earth because of the hatred you have held in your hearts for others without the slightest bit of remorse. I am making your lands desolate and destroying those idols you worship in place of Me. I am making your homes a place where only wild beasts can roam peacefully."

God brought his word against the Persians, saying, "Iran, I am going to break the power of your leadership. I will destroy your mighty army that lives to fight against Me. From all directions I am sending a storm into your land to destroy your political might. I will scatter those who oppose Me in your country to nations who do not face your plight. You will fall before the enemy who is coming to take your life, because my rage against you waxes hot for the wickedness of your plots. I am setting my throne in Iran as I wipe out all its leaders to reestablish a kingdom that honors Me in this land as it did once before. Therefore, those from Iran, I am coming to bring with Me to heaven's door: do not fear, Iran shall be restored."

CHAPTER 50

God turned his attention to the spirit of Nebuchadnezzar and his armies, saying, "United Nations and all you represent, you are destroyed. Your power has been broken. I am breaking up your unity and casting your plans down. The day I have waited for has come to wipe you out forever. With your departure comes the awakening of my people of Israel. They shall come weeping and praising Me for the deliverance from all their enemies. They shall begin flooding back to my land. My people of Israel have been lost sheep. Their political and spiritual leaders have led them astray. They have searched throughout the world to find rest for their souls, when all they have to do is turn their hearts back to Me. Through the ages, they have been consumed by the enemy who has tried to destroy them. Some in the Christian church have said, 'I am the chosen one, and the Jew is not worthy to live.' However, I have never turned away from those who are my chosen.

"Behold, I am raising up an army to judge the spirit of Nebuchadnezzar and his forces that will punish them for their sins. Their pride and disdain of their fellow man has brought shame to those who bore them. I am bringing their existence to an end through a terrifying destruction that will leave all who witness this in great awe. I am surrounding this Babylon with an army to punish it for its sins, and I will leave nothing standing to remind Me of all it did to stir my anger. All its forces will be split and returned to their own lands to never rise again to punish the nations I have given them for this brief time I give them power.

"Israel was first scattered by the might of the Assyrians, and then

I gave them over to the power of the Chaldeans. This same spirit has risen again to afflict the Jewish homeland, but now I say no more, the Babylonian spirit has fallen. I have made a search to find what lies in the hearts of my Jewish people, and now I can finally declare they are clean and totally forgiven.

"I am calling on the enemy to come into Babylon's kingdom with the sound of war and destruction accompanying everywhere he goes. Babylon, this spirit of Nebuchadnezzar and all that he commands has fallen, and his power will be no more. I have laid traps for Babylon of which it is not aware, exposing the sin that resides in its heart that is as black as night. I have formed the weapons for your destruction, spirit from the land of Chaldea. I will destroy you utterly and will make sure you will never be able to recover. The day of my vengeance has arrived to destroy you for your sins. I will not spare as I pass my vengeance on you for attacking my word and my people. I call on the enemy to place a siege on the United Nations and give back to it what it has tried to do to others. This leadership of dictators and all that hate my word has been given power for a day but is now being punished for its war against Me. The men you have controlled and the youth you have propagandized are dead, lying in the streets, victims of your rebellion. Babylon, I am against you and will crush your pride. I will leave you with no one around with whom you can ask for help in your day of judgment.

"All my people who have fallen into captivity by this dictator, the spirit of Nebuchadnezzar will find their Redeemer, the Holy One of Israel who shall release you from his grasp. It is by my hand you will be freed to escape his tyrannical hold. My sword of punishment is reserved to search out and destroy all the leaders of Nebuchadnezzar's government—they are liars and high-ranked men in this consortium of evil. I am moving against his armies and weaponry, bringing in my thieves to steal away his defenses. Their bank accounts and all their finances will be cleaned out to dislodge all their attempts to resist the enemy.

"Oh, Babylon, your wealth has perished, vanquished by the drought, and I am making you fodder for the enemy to be consumed in total, leaving nothing left to grow. I am bringing an enemy from all coasts across the world with a vast and huge army to frighten you into submission. He will come toward you with a very powerful armada and make all your forces run from him in terror. Your king, oh, Babylon, will shake in horror at the report of this approaching army and will rise to fight against this foe but will not be able to prosper. I am publishing to the world the barrenness of Chaldea. The world now sees and hears the cries of the mighty child of Satan."

CHAPTER 51

"Oh, Babylon, I am raising up a very mighty wind to destroy your powerful forces. My wind shall scatter your forces, leaving you empty and barren to the destructive might of the enemy coming to tear you down. Because of your hatred for my people, those who fight for you will be dislodged and feel the wrath of the bloodthirsty weapons formed for this day of my vengeance. Your men shall fall in the streets, and joy shall fill the hearts of my chosen as they watch this massacre take place. The mighty Babylon and all its forces have fallen on the day of my wrath.

"Oh, Babylon, you were the one chosen to bring vengeance on the nations who had forsaken Me, but today is your day to feel my ire because of your allegiance to Satan. Where is the medicine Babylon can take to avoid my coming wrath? It cannot be found, and so everyone must flee this Babylon whom I have ordained to be punished. The armies are being raised to meet the forces that Babylon has been able to muster. However, Babylon must fall and shall not be able to defeat this army coming to pick it clean. Oh, Babylon, set up your defenders to try to withstand the army that is fast approaching, but let all your people know who you control, they are meeting the day of their Armageddon.

"Your heart is full of adultery, and you worship many gods. You have raped the countries of all their wealth, and now your end has come. How can you, O, Babylon, withstand the mighty God? It was I who formed this world through my wisdom and laid the heavens out. It was I who ordered the rain patterns and told the lightning where to strike. The wind has its assignments where to go throughout the width of the earth, and when its circuits have been completed, they start again to encircle the world according to my word.

"Man was formed by Me, and yet he continues to stumble by following false gods that cannot hear, see, or speak. Why do you seek that thing which cannot hear one single prayer or know what desires you have? You are chasing after puffs of air that are gone in less than a second. It is I who defends my people and punishes those who defy my will. It is I who will punish this Babylon for chasing after gods to which they pray to increase the extent of their power. It is my hand that is coming to break in pieces the nations. For defiance against Me and the people who have my protection, armies are being dissolved and crushed while families are split apart. The old and the young, the worker and the employer, and all the ruling elite are meeting their end for being a part of this Babylonian worldly system. I am against you, oh, Babylon, for your lust of power. I am building an altar with you as the sacrifice to end your days on the earth. I am casting you away out of my sight to be like trash thrown away and forgotten.

"I am calling on the nations to prepare. Gather your armies and march on Babylon to destroy this wayward power. Move in on it and crush its people, casting aside all its allies to face my judgment alone.

Kill its armies and scatter its men who wish to fight and defend it. Look in the holes and in the caves to root out all who wish to abet it. Your mighty prince, oh, Babylon, is watching all this destruction. He sees the city he wants to defend fall and his army defeated. The time of your visitation is upon you. The time of harvest for the evil you have sown has reached the time for the reaping.

"The spirit of Nebuchadnezzar has come from the United States to devour all in his path. He has devoured all the wealth the nations could hold, like a parasite feeding on its host. Now is the time to return his own sins back to him with a doubling of his reward. The blood he has spilled has cried out to Me from the earth, hasting the return of my vengeance on him. I will cut off his supply of money and expend all his wealth to leave him defenseless before Me. I am leaving him no man to aid him and rescue his socialist party. I will disband his advisers, and the elite who worship him are going to meet their Waterloo. You are defeated,

Nebuchadnezzar, your armies no longer exist. I am plundering you of all your money and stripping you of all your power.

"Babylon has become a wonder to the nations. This father spirit of the United Nations is being led to the sacrifice like a lamb to the slaughter. Its armies are scattered and dissolved, making it easy for its enemies to plunder. It is dying and being removed to never rise to power again. This Babylon attacked and plundered the country from which my gospel was spread around the world. It has set its heart against the Jew to take from them the land I have given them. For all this, Babylon must pay the price and be slain for its countless murders. Babylon, you will repay: I require your blood for the blood you have spilled of others. My punishment will be swift and start with my judgment of what gods fill your heart. I will expose these gods and cast them away to be burned in the fire of my wrath. If you could build a wall that reached beyond the sky, I would still breach your defenses and set spoilers to loot and defeat you. There is a sound of mourning by those whose hearts are in alignment with the spirit of this wicked Babylon. They cry for the loss of its armies and the removal of its ruling class. My judgment has come upon this clique of men who see themselves as stewards for the world. They think they know what is best for men, but instead, they always chase after what is best for them. Babylon, I am tearing down your walls of defense so no one will be able to help you escape the day of your destruction."

God brought his word to the rulers of Babylon, saying, "I have sent my word against this organization of states to paralyze it and cut it off from my presence. I will destroy your power, your armies, and your wealth and will make the memory of you fade away forever."

CHAPTER 52

God brought his closing words, saying, "I destroyed the last of the kingdom of Judah in 586 BC with the fall of Jerusalem. King Zedekiah fled the city to escape after an eighteen-month siege in complete disobedience of my commands to him. I told him to give himself up to the Chaldeans, but he would not listen. Jerusalem could have been spared from its total destruction if my commands had been obeyed.

"The United States is in the same position today. Obey Me, and your country will not be destroyed by my coming wrath. Continue to live in rebellion against Me, and there is but one remedy for your sins. This book has been written at my command to get the last of my warnings out to you to turn from your sins and repent. I have given you much, and now much is required of you to avoid what is fast approaching. I call on my church to repent. It is they who have remained silent and let this evil fester and grow. The sinner who does not know Me only continues to do what he knows to do. He sins, because that is all he knows. My church, however, has no excuse for its sin. My Son paid the price for your sins with his blood to give you a relationship with Me. It is your prayers and your actions that can give your country redemption. You have disregarded my words and my commands and let this country commit evils and abominations I can no longer abide. Sodom and Gomorrah fell into my judgment because there was no intercessor for them in those cities. This nation will fall because my church has not interceded for this country to save it from my wrath. You cannot pray for this country and continue to live the same lives you have been living and expect Me to honor your prayers.

"If you want godly men holding political office, then you must vote for godly men. If you do not have godly men run for political office, then you are left with the ungodly to rule. You have disobeyed Me by staying out of the political theater. You have disobeyed Me by not going into law and becoming judges. I have called many, but few have heeded my call on their lives. They wish to pursue their own desires in defiance of Me. Therefore, the day of my wrath is at the door ready to strike this country down. Repent now and turn from your wicked ways, or the end of this country has come. I place into your hands power to reverse everything that is befalling this country. The leaders you have now are the ones you elected. They do not know Me and will continue to practice the evil that proceeds out of their hearts. You have listened to their words and believed them, but deceit fills their hearts. You are reaping today what you have sown.

"Call on Me now, those who can hear. Turn your hearts back to Me and obey my words. My church has abandoned Me and has filled itself up with ministers and congregations who do not believe the words I have placed in the Bible. Because they do not believe, they have laid out their own new laws to justify their sins. They are in love with their sins and will die in their sins when the day of my wrath comes. America and my church must turn from their sins now, or this nation will meet its end. The foundation has been laid. There is a new ruler in America whose power will increase to bring about your destruction. I give you a choice to obey my words and go to your neighbor and minister to them my word. When I call you to serve Me in the government and the courts, you must heed my commands. When it is time to vote to place Me as the head of this country, then you must vote for my servants whom I have called to run for these offices. It is time to stop listening to the lies and the promises made to deceive. It is time to follow the guidance of my Holy Spirit and take back what the enemy has stolen. Today is the day of salvation if you heed all of my words, or today is the day of your destruction if you refuse to obey my words."